Bernard Shaw

MICHAEL HOLROYD

Volume 4 · 1950 –1991
The Last Laugh

PENGUIN BOOKS

PENGUIN BOOKS

Published by the Penguin Group
Penguin Books Ltd, 27 Wrights Lane, London W8 5TZ, England
Penguin Books USA Inc., 375 Hudson Street, New York, New York 10014, USA
Penguin Books Australia Ltd, Ringwood, Victoria, Australia
Penguin Books Canada Ltd, 10 Alcorn Avenue, Toronto, Ontario, Canada M4V 3B2
Penguin Books (NZ) Ltd, 182–190 Wairau Road, Auckland 10, New Zealand

Penguin Books Ltd, Registered Offices: Harmondsworth, Middlesex, England

First published as *Volume 4: The Last Laugh* by Chatto & Windus 1992
Published with a revised postscript and new Appendix D (as part of
Volumes 4 & 5: The Shaw Companion) by Chatto & Windus 1992
Published in Penguin Books 1993
1 3 5 7 9 10 8 6 4 2

The title on page iii is set in Caslon Old Face, the
design favoured by Bernard Shaw when he was directing
the manufacture of his books at R. & R. Clark, Edinburgh.
The text is set in Linotron Ehrhardt, a typeface derived
from similar seventeenth-century Dutch sources such as Caslon Old Face.

The moral right of the author has been asserted

Printed in England by Clays Ltd, St Ives plc

PENGUIN BOOKS

BERNARD SHAW
VOLUME 4: 1950–1991

Praise for Michael Holroyd's biography:

'It is, in every sense, a spectacular piece of work ... instantly recognizable as a brilliant *commedia* from the elegant master-hand that cast the spell of *Lytton Strachey* and *Augustus John* ... a feat of style as much as of research, which will surely make it a flamboyant new landmark in modern English life-writing' – Richard Holmes in *The Times*

'No one will ever surpass Holroyd's achievement: it is a balanced, muscular, comprehensive, explanatory, beautifully written life story, composed with an unfaltering integrity, a firm elegance, a shrewd wisdom' – Bernard Levin in *The Times*

'[A] hugely rewarding and informative biography ... A richly satisfying feast for anyone who wants to learn about the man and the mind behind those millions of eloquent words on everything under the sun' – Anthony Curtis in the *Financial Times*

'A man whose art rested so much upon the exercise of intelligence could not have chosen a more intelligent biographer ... The pursuit of Bernard Shaw has grown, and turned into a pursuit of the whole twentieth century' – Peter Ackroyd

'Will rank with the finest biographies of the century. A great life deserves a great Life; Shaw provided the first and Holroyd has hit the bull's-eye with the second ... admirable, extraordinary' – Robertson Davies in the *International Herald Tribune*

Michael Holroyd, who was born in 1935, is half-Swedish and partly Irish. He studied science at Eton College and read literature at the Maidenhead Public Library. He has written biographies of Hugh Kingsmill, Lytton Strachey (Penguin, 1971) and Augustus John (Penguin, 1976). The first three volumes of his biography of Bernard Shaw, *The Search for Love*, *The Pursuit of Power* and *The Lure of Fantasy*, are also published by Penguin. He has been Chairman of the Society of Authors and of the Book Trust, and President of English PEN. He is also a member of the Arts Council and chairs its literature panel. In 1989 he was awarded the CBE for services to literature. He is married to Margaret Drabble.

The Shaw Companion by Michael Holroyd, containing all the Source Notes to his complete biography of Bernard Shaw and a Cumulative Index is published in hardback by Chatto & Windus. Copies of *The Shaw Companion* are obtainable from all good bookshops. In case of difficulty, contact Grantham Book Services Ltd, Isaac Newton Way, Alma Park Industrial Estate, Grantham, Lincs NG31 9SD (tel. 0476 47421)

CONTENTS

Preface   vii

The Shaw Alphabet Reading Key   viii
Androcles and the Lion: Prologue   x

THE LAST LAUGH   1

[1] Two Old Testaments   3
[2] Some Authorized Revisions   26
[3] The National Trust and the Shaw Society   41
[4] Posthumous Appearances forty years on   54
Postscript   85

APPENDICES
A: Charlotte Shaw's Will   91
B: Bernard Shaw's Will   101
C: Principal Purchases from the Shaw Fund by
the National Gallery of Ireland   117
D: List of Films made from Shaw's Works   119

Acknowledgements   127

Index   129

PREFACE

Money is the most important thing in the world.
Preface to *Major Barbara*

'I wish that there could also come later the posthumous life of Shaw,' wrote Anthony Burgess when reviewing my apparently final volume on G.B.S. in *The Observer*. He wanted 'the saga of the estate, the failure of the alphabetic project, the success of *My Fair Lady* which, we've been told, ravaged Shaw's financial afterlife with fantastic and ruinous imposts'. *The Last Laugh*, following the tributaries of two Last Wills and Testaments, attempts to trace that sequel. It is a biography of Shaw's afterlife: a non-fiction, Anglo-Irish comedy of novella length showing how a writer's aspirations and those of his wife were ingeniously diverted in the crosscurrents of modern market economies.

'You would certainly think anyone mad if he claimed to own the air or the sunlight of the sea,' Shaw wrote in the 1920s. Sixty years later it is perhaps G.B.S. who looks rather mad after a decade of privatization. The very frontiers of privacy have moved. There is greater secrecy now surrounding people's financial commitments than their personal relationships. When I began this biography in the mid-1970s I believed that I was writing a work of cultural history. As 'Victorian values' were partially re-introduced, however, many of the social issues over which Shaw had campaigned began to be refought. Latterly he achieved the Shavian position of being simultaneously successful and discredited. He remains controversial. By current standards you cannot ignore a writer whose estate makes almost half-a-million pounds a year more than forty years after his death.

In some respects this epilogue is a peculiarly English narrative. Set amid the persisting legal fogs that fill *Bleak House*, it points parenthetically to the financial adjustments and social conceits of a country in historical decline, plots some awkward connections between yesterday's patronage and today's sponsorship, and follows the mysterious wanderings of individual quixotry through a dense world of business ethics.

Finally it reminds us of the brevity of our collective memory.

The Shaw Alphabet

The letters are classified as Tall,
Beneath each letter is its full name :

Tall :

peep	tot	kick	fee	thigh

Deep :

bib	dead	gag	vow	they

Short :

loll	mime	if	egg	ash

roar	nun	eat	age	ice

Compound :

are	or	air	err

The four most frequent words are represented
Proper names may be distinguished by a
Punctuation and numerals are unchanged. Learn

Reading Key

Deep, Short, and Compound.
its *sound* is shown in **bold** type.

so	sure	**ch**urch	**y**ea	hu**ng**
zoo	mea**s**ure	**j**udge	**w**oe	**h**a-ha
ad**o**	**o**n	w**oo**l	**ou**t	**ah**
up	**oa**k	**oo**ze	**oi**l	**aw**e
array	**ear**	**I**an	**yew**

by single letters: **the** ℘, **of** ʃ, **and** ⱱ, **to** 1.
preceding ' Namer ' dot : e.g. ·ↄoʃ, Rome.
the alphabet *in pairs*, as listed for Writers overleaf.

ANDROCLES AND THE LION

PROLOGUE

Overture: forest sounds, roaring of lions, Christian hymn faintly.

A jungle path. A lion's roar, a melancholy suffering roar, comes from the jungle. It is repeated nearer. The lion limps from the jungle on three legs, holding up his right forepaw, in which a huge thorn sticks. He sits down and contemplates it. He licks it. He shakes it. He tries to extract it by scraping it along the ground, and hurts himself worse. He roars piteously. He licks it again. Tears drop from his eyes. He limps painfully off the path and lies down under the trees, exhausted with pain. Heaving a long sigh, like wind in a trombone, he goes to sleep.

Androcles and his wife Megaera come along the path. He is a small, thin, ridiculous little man who might be any age from thirty to fifty-five. He has sandy hair, watery compassionate blue eyes, sensitive nostrils, and a very presentable forehead; but his good points go no further: his arms and legs and back, though wiry of their kind, look shrivelled and starved. He carries a big bundle, is very poorly clad, and seems tired and hungry.

His wife is a rather handsome pampered slattern, well fed and in the prime of life. She has nothing to carry, and has a stout stick to help her along.

THE LAST LAUGH

1950–1992

Concerning the dead
Nothing ill should be said
So of Shaw let us say:-

> To an age in decay
> He was prophet and priest,
> Providing the yeast
> For the dough of our doubt;
> So puffing it out
> It *appeared* to make bread
> And we *seemed* to be fed.
> His dream was that we
> Could be equal and free
> By dictator's decree

G.B.S. ... R.I.P.

Colin Hurry, November 1950

'Well, now as to practical matters. You may have an idea that Ive flung my money about; but I havnt: I'm richer today than when I first came into the property. Ive used my knowledge of the world to invest my money in ways that other men have overlooked; and whatever else I may be, I'm a safe man from the money point of view.'

Mrs Warren's Profession, Act III

THE LAST LAUGH

I

All mercantile transactions were accompanied with music, so that
they were called Musical Banks...
Samuel Butler, *Erewhon*

Shaw's will, when it was published in March 1951, turned out to be a most unpopular document. 'Had he deliberately set out to ensure that the least possible profit should accrue to future generations from his wealth,' commented *The Economist*, 'it is hard to see how he could have done better.' Several newspapers carried the same incredulous headline: 'Left a fortune for reform of alphabet.' It seemed as prodigiously silly as anything since Labiche's statistician set out to enumerate the widows crossing the Pont Neuf.

The gross value of his estate amounted to £367,233 (equivalent to £5,000,000 in 1990). It was an extraordinary sum for a writer: Thomas Hardy had left £91,000 in 1928; G. K. Chesterton £28,000 in 1936; J. M. Barrie £173,500 in 1937; H. G. Wells £60,000 in 1946. In due course an assessment of his copyrights would have to be added to Shaw's estate, and since G.B.S. himself had calculated that these copyrights 'may run into six figures', the total fortune had every chance of rising to a glittering £500,000. What was to become of this spectacular wealth, largely accumulated over the years from money spent by the public on books and theatre tickets? Apparently it had been fool's gold, an old fool's gold, and was posthumously reverting to base metal. People felt the same sense of loss as if they had been tricked out of a lawful prize. Such squandering struck them as unpardonable in the early 1950s.

The British public had been living through more than a decade of austerity which only now was coming to an end with the final lifting of food rationing and the long-awaited opening of the Festival of Britain. Six million people paid five shillings to step from a past world of grey skies and khaki clothing, export rejects, bomb sites, into the bright new architecture of coloured festival pavilions with dazzling murals and futuristic shapes topped by a filigree 'Skylon' tower taller than any building in London and prevented from taking off into the heavens, it appeared, by its almost invisible cables. At the centre of the festival, like a science fiction vision, stood the miraculous Dome of Discovery. Aeronautical technology developed in the war was suddenly being put to domestic and industrial use. People wondered whether this was a mirage of Modernism or the blueprint for a new world.

To recover from post-war 'hunger, poverty, desperation and chaos', Britain had borrowed over $2,500,000,000 in Marshall aid from the United States, more than any other European country. By the beginning of 1951 her overseas trade enabled her to dispense with further borrowing, yet she appeared to have traded away part of her sovereignty. The cultural, educational and intellectual practices in which Shaw had sought to invest his posthumous copyright income were to be eroded by the need to make Britain's academies, galleries and museums part of an expanding entertainment industry. With its thirty acres of pleasure gardens and fun fairs in Battersea, the Festival of Britain would retrospectively look more like a theme park for tourists than a commemoration of the Great Exhibition that in 1851 had converted its profits into funds for scholarships.

It was the worst of times for financing scholarship in the arts and humanities. Many Americans felt they had already sent over more than they could afford, while everyone in Britain needed to spend money on themselves. Nevertheless a Shaw Memorial Fund was set up in 1951, its objects being to subsidize young authors, dramatists and musicians, encourage the 'worthy presentation' of Shaw's own plays at festivals, and maintain the fabric of Shaw's Corner which he had given to the National Trust without an endowment. Though these aims were more acceptable than reforming the alphabet, the public did not see why it should have to pay for them when there was so much of Shaw's own money apparently going to waste. 'I regret that the public should be asked, at this time, to subscribe a quarter of a million pounds to undertake three enterprises, one of which is unnecessary, the second of which is unimportant, and the third of which is dangerous,' wrote Rebecca West. '. . . I do not know why such a fund . . . should be associated with the name of Bernard Shaw, who preferred to help literature in another way and had a right to do so if he chose.' The fact that Clement Attlee, the Prime Minister, was associating himself with the campaign, together with a rumour that it was to have the support of the Labour Government, made the venture all the more untimely. Following some hesitation, its opening was delayed until

. after the general election which that October swept Attlee from office and returned the Conservatives to power. Within a few days all the Festival of Britain structures except the Concert Hall were dismantled, leaving people wondering whether this new architecture had been built to last like 'proper' buildings in the past, or even the tower blocks and symmetrical housing estates that were spreading round them; or alternatively whether it had merely been a collection of adult toys.

On 23 November, the new Chancellor of the Exchequer R. A. Butler (who that year was elected President of the Royal Society of Literature and later created Baron Butler of Saffron Walden) launched the appeal as 'a world tribute to Shaw's memory'. He looked forward to some 'spectacular donations', for 'if there was to be a tribute to Shaw it must be on a worthy scale'.

'A passable Shavian comedy could be worked up out of the meeting held this afternoon to open the Shaw memorial appeal,' reported the *Manchester Guardian*. Almost at once the proceedings were splattered with confusion. Lady Astor got to her feet and described how she had implored G.B.S. on his deathbed to renounce his alfabet trusts. She appealed to the Chancellor of the Exchequer 'to break that ridiculous will', adding darkly that the money would be better spent in establishing a society to save Shaw 'from his so-called friends'. Her outburst appeared in all the national newspapers. The actor Sir Lewis Casson also took the floor, accusing the National Trust of making 'a great mistake' in accepting Shaw's 'dreadful house'. Lewis had been Drama Director of the Council for the Encouragement of Music and the Arts (CEMA, the precursor of the Arts Council) and, until recently, President of British Actors' Equity. His opinions were also widely reported. Finally Marie Stopes pleaded for the money to be used instead for a life-size statue of G.B.S. in Adelphi Gardens, and the meeting broke up discordantly leaving Shaw's biographer St John Ervine 'full of doubts and disapproval'.

'I do not know of any precedent for such a tribute to the memory of any man of letters,' cautioned T. S. Eliot. '... The work of Mr Shaw is not likely to be forgotten. Several of his plays should certainly be included in the repertory of a National Theatre; they will, in any case, be performed so long as England retains any pride in its theatre. I cannot see why the plays of Mr Shaw, simply for their dramatic merit, should enjoy an advantage over the plays of Shakespeare, Jonson, Congreve, Yeats and Synge, among which some of them already have an assured place.' The target was £250,000 (equivalent to more than £3,000,000 in 1990) and the total eventually reached £416 (£6,000 in 1990). It was 'a complete failure and a disastrous flop', lamented Archibald Henderson.

Yet Shaw's finances were not quite what the public perceived them to be. The net value of his estate was £301,585 of which £180,571 became immediately due in death duties. Nor was this all. Once the copyrights had been valued, 70 per cent of this notional amount would have to be paid in additional death duties. Besides this, there were more than a dozen annuities in Shaw's will, mostly bequests to those who had worked for him at Ayot and in London, which had to be met each year. Since his royalties were bringing in less than £50,000 a year, and might soon decrease (his earliest plays shortly coming out of copyright in the United States), there seemed a likelihood that the alfabet trusts, which were confined to twenty-one years from his death so as to avoid the legal taint of perpetuity, would be largely washed out. No one could tell what would happen. Towards the end of 1951 public attention turned to what the *Star* called 'The "Tangled Will" of Mrs Shaw'.

*

Charlotte Shaw had bequeathed £94,000 to Ireland for educational purposes. The main provisions in her will resemble clauses from the five wills Shaw himself made between 1901 and 1937. She wanted the money to be used for three objects: bringing masterpieces of fine art, including music and painting, within the reach of all classes of Irish people; teaching Irish people the secrets of self-control, elocution, oratory and deportment; and the endowment of a Chair or Readership at an Irish University for instruction in these matters of fine art and social intercourse. Her wishes were considered so unusual that the National Provincial Bank, as trustee of her estate, brought the matter before the Chancery Division of the High Court in London to determine whether under English law they constituted a valid charitable trust.

The last day of November 1951 was dubbed 'Irish Day' by the English newspapers. Solicitors and barristers from all the interested parties gathered in the courtroom of Mr Justice Vaisey. The English bank questioned the will, and an Irish bank defended it. The Attorney-General supported it and was himself supported by the Public Trustee on behalf of Bernard Shaw's estate. But lawyers representing Charlotte's next of kin challenged the trusts as being void by reason of remoteness and uncertainty.

Everyone thoroughly agreed on Charlotte's highmindedness. She had made her will in 1937 and after a pause, a pause of fourteen years, it had come for mature examination to Chancery. A murmur of approval went round the court when the judge described it as 'a very interesting document revealing a mind of a very high quality and a lady with every wish to do right'. It was at Chancery because 'the lady seems to have got tangled up in a web of her own verbosity and it makes it very difficult to untangle her'. No one recognized the unconscious pun relating to Sidney Webb who had helped to draft Charlotte's will. They were relishing what they conceived to be the fanciful Shavian circumlocutions of the case. There was laughter in court when his lordship said he detected 'an inspiration which derives from another source, but I must not say where'.

Charlotte's will seemed oddly lacking in the good manners she sought to promote. 'It is not very complimentary to those people she hoped to benefit, is it?' the judge inquired.

'It does occur to me that if a person of Irish domicile were to promote a trust for curing the awkward manners, vulgarities of speech and social impossibilities of English people, then it would be regarded as not very well calculated to add to the friendliness of the nations.'

There was more laughter when Sir Charles Russell, a King's Counsel instructed by the National City Bank (an Irish bank appointed as the ultimate trustee under Charlotte's will), replied: 'quite frankly, my lord, we are prepared to accept these insults.'

The case was to be decided less by legal argument than by the self-control and deportment of contending counsel. Charlotte had bequeathed her niece Cecily Colthurst £20,000 which was paid to her in 1944. But if the court declared a partial intestacy and Charlotte's wishes were blocked, then Mrs Colthurst would inherit the extra £94,000. Here was a case that needed to be presented with delicacy if it were not to appear grasping. But Pascoe Hayward KC, representing Mrs Colthurst, was not delicate. While Sir Charles Russell politely referred to Charlotte as a 'serious-minded lady dealing with a serious subject', Mr Pascoe Hayward called her a 'cranky' person whose large fortune was in danger of being lamentably 'frittered away' by a lot of other 'cranky people'. It would be open to her trustees, he protested, to encourage social intercourse by giving 'a series of cocktail parties'. Were he himself a trustee, he persisted, he would instil self-control by building plenty of good strong nourishing prisons and seeing 'that people who do not control themselves go there'. These trusts were 'doomed to failure', he concluded, for the very proper legal reason that there was no precedent for them. So how could the public benefit? 'There is no evidence that anyone in Ireland – and they do the maddest things in Ireland – has ever tried to instruct anyone in social intercourse.'

'"Finishing School" for the Irish People', announced the *Manchester Guardian* on 4 December. 'Disposal of Mrs Shaw's Money Settled.' Refusing to test the validity of the trusts by presupposing perverse ways of applying them, Mr Justice Vaisey (otherwise Sir Harry Vaisey) decided that under English law Charlotte had kept herself within the necessary limits 'by a rather narrow margin'.

So the money passed out of England into Ireland. 'How the people of Ireland will react to such intensive treatment as Mrs Shaw appears to envisage', Mr Justice Vaisey remarked, 'I ought not to speculate.' But a ripple of delirious speculation was already passing over the twenty-six counties of the Republic. 'Ireland Seeks Shaw Culture', announced the newspapers. '£94,000 Rush For Grants By Mrs G.B.S.' Before long almost a hundred applications had been prepared by universities, cultural groups, local authorities and some enterprising individuals demanding art galleries, gramophone records, endowments for lectures, subsidies for theatres. '£94,000 sounds a lot of money,' parried an official at the National City Bank in Dublin, 'and many of the applicants seem to have dreams of building palaces.' £94,000 *was* a lot of money in the early 1950s, equivalent to a little over £1,000,000 in the early 1990s. People were impatient to show off the flicker and dazzle of their new deportment. But the bands got no new instruments, and no foundations for new libraries were laid. After a year, cultural life in Ireland seemed unchanged; and after two years it was still further unchanged. The National and Municipal Art Galleries in Dublin did not know what was going on, neither did the Royal Academy of Music nor the Dublin School of Art, and their cumulative lack of knowledge was comprehensively shared by the Abbey and Gate theatres. 'Where is the £94,000?' the *News Chronicle* demanded.

There were excellent banking reasons for this inactivity. For until the £94,000 had accrued sufficient interest to make possible grants of 'some £3,000 a year', positively nothing could be done.

The first results of Charlotte's bequest were witnessed in the summer of 1954 at a hostel in Termonfeckin, County Louth, where forty students assembled for a week of instruction by artists, linguists, and the director of a mannequin agency. The successful applicant had been Forás Éireann, an *omnium gatherum* of native 'sons of the soil' formed in 1949 to plant village halls in rural communities. 'The students will be available later to conduct other similar courses throughout the country,' reported the *Irish Independent*. Forás Éireann 'hopes to be able to lend itself further to the purposes of the bequest'. So it was to be...

... and so it still is. Under the Trustees Act of 1893 the National City Bank retired and appointed the Bank of Ireland in its place. But Forás Éireann continues to distribute Charlotte's money as part of its policy for developing rural Ireland in accordance with 'Christian and national ways of life'. No Chair or Readership has been established at any Irish university. After forty years of capitalist expansion and inflation the value of Charlotte's money would have risen to almost £1,250,000 if it had kept level with the cost-of-living index. In fact the size of annual donations suggests that it has fallen dramatically. 'Each year we spend, roughly, about £2,500 to £3,000 under the heading of Art,' writes the Trust organizer at Forás Éireann, 'and this is used to support smaller ventures throughout the twenty-six counties.'

'It is the policy of the Bank,' writes the Bank of Ireland, 'for confidentiality reasons, not to reveal any details about the financial aspect of the Trust.'

Charlotte's grand pretensions, with all the hopes once circling them, had in any case fallen behind a constellation of events that began to cluster and pulse round G.B.S.'s will in the centenary year of his birth.

*

On 15 March 1956 a spectacular musical adaptation of Shaw's phonetic romance *Pygmalion* opened at the Mark Hellinger Theater on Broadway. *My Fair Lady* contained fifteen numbers composed by Frederick Loewe with lyrics by Alan J. Lerner, and it was directed by Moss Hart. Yet the production was in many ways a very English affair. With his irrepressible leer and roguish eye, his stentorian roar, Stanley Holloway played the undeserving dustman Doolittle in a broad style that derived from the old music hall tradition ('With a Little Bit of Luck', 'Get me to the Church on Time'). He incorporated the same ironic cheerfulness he had earlier brought to the gravedigger in *Hamlet*. Stella Campbell's part as the flower girl was taken by the twenty-one-year-old Julie Andrews. Known mostly as a pantomime performer in Britain, she had recently won a devoted American following in *The Boy Friend* and was to complete her conquest of New York by singing and dancing Eliza's new role ('Wouldn't it be Loverly', 'I Could Have Danced All Night') with charming expressiveness. Rex Harrison brought off a histrionic triumph by turning his lack of singing voice into the half-rasping, half-caressing baritone patter of Henry Higgins's 'I'm an Ordinary Man', 'A Hymn to Him' and 'Why Can't the English'. Cecil Beaton's rich costumes, which ranged from a street crowd of raffish cockney buskers to the wheel hats and feathered parasols of Mrs Higgins's fashionable tea-party and the mock-stately black, white and grey pageant of the 'Ascot Gavotte', were to be taken up by New York *couturiers* and judged to be more attractive than all the posters of the British Tourist Board. *My Fair Lady* seemed one of those rare theatrical collaborations in which everyone, working on top form, came harmoniously together. Like the comic operas of Gilbert and Sullivan, like *The Merry Widow*, *Oklahoma!*, *Annie Get Your Gun* and *Me and My Girl* (which also derives from *Pygmalion*), this new musical exerted a lasting attraction. Moss Hart's production was to run on Broadway for 2,717 performances over six and a half years, by which time $55,000,000 had already been made from performances round the world, plus another $10,000,000 from recordings and film rights, breaking all financial records.

Even at the previews in New Haven it was obvious that *My Fair Lady* was destined to be a popular success. This prospect, together with a rise in the number of international performances of Shaw's plays, suddenly brought his six-year-old will into new focus.

*

The Official Trustee Act introduced by the Liberal Government in 1906 had created an official whose advantage over private and commercial trustees was to lie in the certainty that trust funds which he administered would never be embezzled, lost in speculation, or misdirected. Shaw had appointed the Public Trustee as his executrix in a will he made in 1913 and in all subsequent wills. 'I was a strong advocate of a Public Trustee long before 1906,' he wrote.

Referring to Shaw's last will, the Public Trustee Wyndham Hirst (later Sir Wyndham Hirst) had stated in 1951 that his 'primary duty' was to satisfy all legatees and annuitants. Research into the proposed new alfabet was to remain 'a secondary matter' and could be considered 'only if anything is left over'. Owing to the 'very material increases in death duties', there did not appear much danger of serious money being left over. So the alfabet could safely be laid to one side. 'It may be several months, or even years, before we can submit all the valuations necessary for a final assessment,' an official in his department hazarded. For five and a half years, while lodging a 'corrective affidavit' to show additions to the estate, the Public Trustee sat negotiating with the Estate Duty Office. Then, in the spring of 1956, they hit on the figure of £433,500. It was a handsome amount, indeed unprecedented, bringing the net value of Shaw's estate nicely beyond £700,000 (equivalent to £6,250,000 in 1990) and raising the final death duties to a magnificent pinnacle of £524,000 (£4,750,000 in 1990). More than half this sum was due at once and might possibly be swelled by a further generous accretion of interest. Nevertheless, it would still not be a substantial enough obstacle to keep the fearful alfabet long entombed. As the alfabet's custodian, there was only one judicious course of action open to the Public Trustee, and that was to bring the whole matter to Chancery, where it would be placed under the scrutiny of the High Court. On 26 March 1956, eleven days after the successful opening of *My Fair Lady* on Broadway, *The Times* announced in London that the British Museum was to challenge the validity of these alfabet trusts. When a question about Shaw's will was asked in the House of Commons the following month, the Chancellor of the Exchequer, Harold Macmillan (later Lord Stockton), was able to reply that 'the matter is *sub judice* and I can make no statement...'

It was not easy for interested members of the public to find their way to the case when it opened in January 1957. On the Warned List it had appeared somewhat eccentrically as 'Public Trustee v. Day and Others', Fred Day being Shaw's gardener, whose annuity (with that of his wife) was to be reviewed during the first morning. Several wandering Shavians were gathered up and mistakenly conducted to the more glamorous business of Diana Dors, the 'blonde bombshell' who was petitioning for a divorce in another court nearby. Extricating themselves from the crowd, they finally settled into the more reposeful atmosphere of the Lord Chancellor's Court and, during the long implacable afternoon, heard the legal distinction between 'benevolent' and 'philanthropic' begin to drift backwards and forwards over the network of Shaw's Last Will and Testament.

'The Lord Chancellor's Court is Gothic in more than architecture,' observed the *Manchester Guardian*. 'Mr Justice Harman's face in repose

– elongated and narrow-eyed, with the light falling on it from above – might at times have been that of a medieval king in effigy. The lethargy that sometimes overtook the spectators as precedents were unrolled might have put them in mind of something very old and long lasting – the case of Jarndyce v. Jarndyce, say – rather than the quick by-play of the court scenes in "The Devil's Disciple".'

Shaw had believed that the need for alphabetical reform arose from the fact that there were more sounds in the English language than there were letters in its Latin alphabet. Some letters were therefore used to signify more than one sound and the language was choked with illogical two-letter combinations, such as *sh*, *th* and *ng*. This notorious orthography, perverting the natural logic of children's minds, was partly responsible for the high proportion of semi-literates in Britain and had slowed down the spread of English as an international language. English usage was overloaded with unnecessary grammar and tedious penwork. These convictions sprang perhaps from Shaw's own backward years at school and his need to escape deprivation in Ireland.

All this Shaw had argued in his lifetime. But believing his main contribution to the cause of alphabet reform to be that of propaganda, supported by money, he advanced the economic case for reform in his will. 'Write up in letters of gold round your office,' he had instructed James Pitman in 1947, '*England Knows Nothing of Phonetics, Hates Education, But Will Do Anything For Money*.' Having found no public department or learned society to nominate as the executant of his easy alfabet, he had been obliged to create two private trusts. The first was designed to find out, by means of statistical inquiry, how much time could be saved by people who spoke the English language and wrote it using the proposed alfabet, thereby showing the extent of time and labour wasted by the use of the present alphabet, and then, if possible, to make a calculation of this waste in terms of loss of money. The second trust was to transliterate *Androcles and the Lion* into the phonetic alfabet, assuming a given pronunciation of English, to publish and advertise this transliteration in a special bi-alphabetic edition with the existing alphabet on one side and the proposed alfabet on the other, and so by the dissemination of copies in public libraries and by the general debate this would give rise to, persuade the Government or public or English-speaking world to adopt it.

The legal machinery used by the Chancery Division of the High Court of Justice to test the validity of Shaw's trusts was the Preamble to the Statute of Queen Elizabeth I. Of the five categories of charity there enumerated, two appeared *prima facie* applicable to this case: the third category which was education, and the fourth category which was public utility.

There were four parties represented in court. The Attorney-General was in it *parens patriae*, as the official protector of charities. His counsel, Mr E. Milner Holland QC (later Sir Edward Milner Holland) contended that the trusts were legal charities and could not be invalidated for unenforceability or uncertainty since the Charity Commissioners might modify them if necessary to see that the testator's wishes were carried out in spirit even if they could not be carried out to the letter. The Public Trustee was in it as Shaw's executor. Though unable to conceal his personal opinion that these alfabetical matters were a lot of poppycock, he argued through his counsel, Mr Robert Lazarus, that even if the trusts were not charitable, he should be allowed to carry out the provisions of Shaw's bequest. The British Museum and the Royal Academy of Dramatic Art were in it as ultimate residuary legatees and had instructed Sir Charles Russell QC – the same Charles Russell who had so successfully fought for Charlotte's Irish trust over five years earlier – to contest the validity of these alfabetical trusts. The third residuary legatee, the National Gallery of Ireland, had engaged Mr K. E. Elphinstone *not* to contest the validity of the trusts. 'Is that in order to put the court in a greater difficulty by having no help from you, or what?' inquired Mr Justice Harman. To which Mr Elphinstone replied that the Governor and Guardians of the National Gallery of Ireland 'did not want to put forward any argument to defeat the intention of a very distinguished fellow-Irishman in a matter very dear to his heart'. He did not explain that, Irish charity laws being stricter than English, his participation might imperil the contestants' claim.

The residuary legatees were in a very favourable position, for even if they lost the case, all Shaw's royalties after 1971 would still automatically become theirs. But if they won it, the royalties would go to them immediately in three equal portions. 'They may be likened to a school-boy who has a half-share in a bottle of pop, half of which gets spilt when the bottle is opened, and who proceeds to drink all that is left because *his* half-share was at the bottom,' wrote Barbara Smoker, a founder member of the Phonetic Alphabet Association. 'Not content with having the comparatively safe bottom half of the Shaw residue, the British Museum and the Royal Academy of Dramatic Art have also been claiming in the Chancery Court whatever can be salvaged of the top half – which will be so much more now than seemed likely a year ago.'

There were seldom more than thirty members of the public in court – mainly a scattering of intellectual-looking old gentlemen, some middle-aged women in astrakhan collars and brown hats, a few young Indian and Scandinavian students of British justice. There was also the thirty-three-year-old Barbara Smoker.

Barbara Smoker occupied two attic rooms without inside sanitation on Catford Hill. She was a freethinker, ate very little meat, and bought her clothes mainly at jumble sales. Barbara Smoker had no job, but made a meagre living by winning competitions – literary competitions and competitions on the backs of tins and packets for slogans, jingles, ditties – with a little journalism besides.

Barbara Smoker had no job but she was always busy. On Thursdays, for example, she could be heard on her soap box at Tower Hill contra-dicting what the Methodist minister Donald Soper (later Baron Soper) had been saying on Wednesdays. She was a passionate campaigner, coherent, courageous, iconoclastic, unconquerable in her crusade against the Big Lie of religion. For forty years she was to persist, without a job, working round the clock as Chairman of the Voluntary Euthanasia Society, President of the National Secular Society, a champion of the Family Squatting Movement, a force within the Radical Alternatives to Prison Committee.

She had come to the Chancery Court in her dual role as secretary of the Phonetic Alphabet Association and assistant secretary of the Shaw Society. It had not been easy. When Shaw's solicitors informed her they were allowed to divulge no information whatever, not even the date of the hearing, she took to telephoning the Public Trustee; and when she found he was never in his office, she wrote him letters which though acknowledged were never answered. Finally she had gone to the court itself, made friends with an official there, and arranged to speak to him each day until the case opened.

The setting and proceedings promised 'little scope for cut-and-thrust comedy', regretted the *Manchester Guardian*. '. . . Shaw and the Gothic do not mix.' But amid their blue bags and pink ribbons, their intermin-able briefs, learned counsel essayed quite a few comic recitatives. They questioned whether Shaw's name should begin with a *P*. When Charles Russell cited a precedent involving a man who left a legacy to a horse and a dog which the court found was not charitable, Mr Justice Harman objected that there was no horse or dog in Shaw's will. 'No, My Lord, but I submit there is some analogy between a pet animal and a pet hobby.' To which his Lordship conceded: 'I suppose they might both be called hobby-horses.'

Sir Charles Russell was an impressive advocate on behalf of the British Museum and the Royal Academy of Dramatic Art, and his speeches, enriched with many gnarled precedents and crackling Latin tags, made very pretty hearing. Listening to him from the public gallery, it took Barbara Smoker several minutes to realize that no one without prior knowledge of phonetics, and the allied subjects of typography and shorthand, could possibly understand that most of his mellifluous statements were rubbish. It appeared that she was the one person in court who had this purifying knowledge – indeed she was bursting with it. It was crucial that she educate learned counsel. Except for an affidavit from Daniel Jones, the Professor Emeritus of Phonetics at the University of London, and despite some expert advice from Shaw's old colleague James Pitman (whose heart quite frankly was in simplified spelling rather than alphabet reform), the Attorney-General's case sounded pitifully unprepared. Incredible as it seemed, he knew nothing of Jesperson and Zamenhof, or even the difference between inflected and agglutinated language! When Barbara Smoker heard Charles Russell claim that the alfabet trusts would require a change of law because they were analogous to political trusts, when she saw this contention go unchallenged, knowing herself that nothing more would be involved than had been needed for the teaching of shorthand as a supplementary means of writing or the invention of Morse Code, she could bear it no longer. *My Lord!*

But 'there was nothing I could do there and then unless I wanted to risk being sent out of the court.' When the case was adjourned for the day, however, and before it was resumed next morning, she was on to the Attorney-General's counsel, and he could not throw her off. Though she was in her own words 'a mere nobody', Mr E. Milner Holland QC had little option but to receive her evidence.

He had no sense of the avalanche he had set in motion. From the public gallery she descended to the body of the court and into the thick of the fight. Each day with her pens and papers she would set about demolishing the British Museum and the Royal Academy of Dramatic Art. At the end of each day she had amassed thousands of potent words ready to slip into Mr E. Milner Holland's briefcase. She filled his bag with facts – facts about David's *Neuhand*, Kunowski's *Sprechspur*, the Ridge-Beedle design system, the Erhard Roman Augmented and Dewey's work on the relative frequency of English speech sounds. She gave him evidence to study in the evenings on the educational use of phonetic lettering in more than sixty West German schools, and explained why the word 'though' in two letters supported his case while the word 'enough' in four did not. Sometimes, quite often in fact, when especially horrified by the court's ignorance, she could not restrain herself from sending over sheaves of writings to him in court. She was disappointed to find that it was considered bad form for barristers to refer to notes, let alone read out well-prepared arguments. It seemed that everything must appear to flow in a spontaneous stream of inspiration. When some of her points, involving delicate phonetic technicalities, came out strangely garbled, she also discovered that it was impossible for any self-respecting barrister to correct himself. But she wrote on and was pleased to see that by the end of the week, when Mr E. Milner Holland QC opened his tremendously bulging briefcase and she looked into its jaws, over half the material to be digested there was her own.

'Public Trustee v. Day and Others' spread itself over nine days with a three-day adjournment. This was Barbara Smoker's first experience of Chancery. Visiting Mr E. Milner Holland QC in his chambers she was horrified to find him catching up with his other cases. Each night she had been typing out her notes, while he had been merely using his train journeys for the Shaw case. He reassured her somewhat, however, by explaining that he had omitted much of her scholarly advice because it referred to legally irrelevant issues. The fact that these issues were being introduced by opposing counsel was, he added, a sign that the opposition was worried.

The hearing ended with Sir Charles Russell quoting a line from *Androcles and the Lion* – 'Did um get an awful thorn into um's tootsum wootsum?' – and querying whether a phonetic transliteration of this speech would really be charitable. Mr Justice Harman reserved his judgment for four weeks.

*

When making his will Shaw had discovered that his solicitor, unable to credit the alfabet trusts, had drafted the clauses as if they were ingenious devices for tax avoidance. He was therefore obliged to take up the pen and redraft some of these passages himself. What he wrote, though clear enough to the man or woman on the Clapham Omnibus, baffled the lawyers, while the legal repetitions and prolixities of the skilled equity draughtsman looked in their baroque magnificence like gibberish to the ordinary reader. It was an awkward mixture of styles, 'a marriage of incompatibles', admitted Mr Justice Harman when delivering his reserved judgment on 20 February 1957. The 'delicate testamentary machinery devised by the conveyancer could but suffer when subjected to the *cacœthes scribendi* [urge to write] of the author', he regretted, 'even though the latter's language if it stood alone, might be a literary masterpiece'. The long and complicated document had been made when Shaw was in his ninety-fourth year but it 'was rather youthful exuberance than the hesitations of old age that marred its symmetry', his lordship remarked.

Mr Justice Harman did not sound hostile to G.B.S. He described him as 'an indefatigable reformer' who had acted as 'a kind of "itching powder"' to the British public, to the English-speaking peoples and indeed to an even wider audience', bombarding them all with 'such a combination of paradox and wit that he became before his death a kind of oracle – the Shavian oracle'.

English orthography and pronunciation, he continued, were obvious targets for the reformer.

'It was as difficult for the native to defend the one as it was for the foreigner to compass the other. The evidence showed that for many years Shaw had been interested in the subject. Perhaps his best known excursion in the field is *Pygmalion* ... It was indeed a curious reflection that this same work, tagged with versicles which I suppose Shaw would have detested, and tricked out with music, which he would have eschewed ... was now charming huge audiences on the other side of the Atlantic and had given birth to the present proceedings ... receipts from this source had enabled the executor at length to get on terms with the enormous death duties payable on the estate, thus bringing the interpretation of the will into the realm of practical politics.'

Mr Justice Harman took more than an hour to read his judgment. 'Who was to say whether this project was beneficial?' he asked. The answer, of course, was that Mr Justice Harman was to say. He confessed to some reluctance in preventing a man disposing of his own money as he thought fit. Nevertheless this was what he was going to do. He was 'not at liberty' to confer a halo of charity on the trusts because they appeared merely 'to tend to the increase of public knowledge'. In the end it was excruciatingly simple. The trusts were for an object rather than a person and an object could not complain to Chancery which therefore was not able to control the trust and so would not allow it to continue. Consequently the will created neither a valid charitable trust, his lordship concluded, nor a valid unenforceable trust. Both trusts therefore being void, the three residuary legatees were entitled to come into their inheritance at once – as soon as all legal expenses had been settled.

This summing-up pleased the lawyers. Mr Justice Harman, they reminded themselves, was himself an Irishman. They congratulated him on blending law and literature in a brilliant pastiche of Shaw's lucid style that 'will hold its place in any company in any age', stated Lord Birkett. Two years later Mr Justice Harman was created Lord Justice Harman, and in 1961 his judgment found a place in *The Law as Literature: An Anthology of Great Writing in and about the Law* published by The Bodley Head, which not long afterwards took over from Constable as the publishers of Shaw's own work.

It was a setback, Shavians agreed, but hardly a defeat. In the 1940s, having read of a Chancery judge who ruled as invalid a bequest leaving the testator's property to community centres and handed the money instead to the next of kin, Shaw had accepted that he must run a similar risk. 'If nothing happens, or the bequest fails through any cause', he wrote to James Pitman in the summer of 1944, 'I have provided alternative destinations for the money which will prevent its being "left in the air" in any case.'

'I cannot guard against litigation over my definition of a British alphabet; but as I attach much more importance to advertisement of the need for the alphabet than to the success of my attempt to provide it my ghost will be perfectly satisfied if the lawyers and litigants keep the subject in the headlines for the twenty years' perpetuity limit.'

The two stalwarts in this business of keeping Shaw's alfabet in the headlines were Barbara Smoker and the half-Irish Old Etonian publisher and educationist James Pitman. One in Catford, the other in Chelsea, they formed an odd but admirable team. Pitman, then in his young fifties, was an engagingly eclectic character who had been an international athlete, director of the Bank of England and for the last dozen years Conservative Member of Parliament for Bath. 'He was not very quick on the uptake,' Barbara Smoker severely noted, and he wrote 'in the most appalling Pitman shorthand I had ever seen'. He would end each day in chaos, but all was smoothed back into order next morning by his perfect secretary, Miss Blisset. Spelling reform circulated in Pitman's blood: it was his love, and eventually his infatuation.

It was amazing to Pitman that the judge had found his way to such a consummate misinterpretation of Shaw's clearly expressed intentions. It was equally amazing that the Attorney-General had no wish to appeal. As soon as the judgment had been given, Pitman called a press conference under his own name and that of his fellow dare-devil Barbara Smoker. The costs of the Chancery case were estimated at between £6,000 and £10,000 and an appeal would require over £3,000 more. Apparently undeterred by the fate of the Shaw Memorial Fund six years earlier, Pitman suggested opening a public subscription, to be managed by the Shaw Society, which would facilitate the appeal or alternatively assist the implementation of Shaw's wishes privately. In confidence Pitman told the Shaw Society that if the subscription failed he would put up the money himself.

The press conference was well attended and became front-page news when journalists later reported that Pitman had been rebuked for holding it by the Attorney-General Sir Reginald Manningham-Buller (then nicknamed Sir Reginald Bullying-Manner, and later created Viscount Dilhorne). This vexing business was beginning to plague the Attorney-General. He wished it would go away. Instead he was obliged to issue a statement reminding the press that James Pitman was not a party to the case. They had spoken 'casually' in the Division Lobby at Westminster, and the Attorney-General felt distressed that their conversation, being 'of an informal, confidential, and private character', should have been made public. It was breaching club rules. Naturally he would appeal if there were grounds for doing so. But, of course, there weren't. On 7 May the two of them clashed again, this time in public on the floor of the House of Commons, and their irritated exchanges occupied twelve columns of Hansard's official report, further appeasing Shaw's ghost.

James Pitman and Barbara Smoker disagreed on many things. They disagreed on the conduct of the case in Chancery, on the legitimate grounds for an appeal, and on the conflicting merits of simplified spelling versus phonetic reform. But they campaigned together in confident Shavian style. While he kept matters boiling in the House of

Commons, bending some ears and boxing others, she composed press statements from her lair in the Shaw Society which were quoted in news bulletins and reproduced in *The Times*. She did more: throwing out many thousands of words, loaded with research findings, in lectures, articles, and unanswered correspondence to the Attorney-General. 'But I do not kid myself that it does very much good,' she admitted.

By the summer they had attracted some unexpected support from the United States. A New York attorney, Mrs Clara Richter, flew into London 'hell bent with a mission from God' to set the English law right. Following a late *levée* at the Dorchester Hotel, *The Times* reported that she would be representing the American Theater Council and had obtained an 'encouraging' legal opinion in London. 'She plainly let it be known what kind of woman the various authorities concerned would be up against,' commented *The Shavian*, 'and quite frankly we think they deserve it.'

The difficulty facing these campaigners was that the public cared nothing for alphabet reform. Fumes of sanctity shrouded the conventions of established language. If shamed and goaded, the public would probably have applauded the anonymous defender of English orthography who, a few days after Shaw's death, had paid the statutory shilling to file a protest against his will on the ground that it would 'gravely affect the majesty of the English language and would have serious repercussions on English literature'.

Barbara Smoker and James Pitman could not reach the Attorney-General but, by somehow keeping it all in the newspapers and by obtaining a counsel's opinion that was not utterly unfavourable, they did force some action out of the Public Trustee who, on the last day allowed, lodged an appeal. His case was the same as it had been in the Chancery Court, namely that the trusts might be valid even if not charitable, and that he should therefore be allowed to carry out Shaw's wishes. Knowing by now that this was an impossible position in law (and influenced perhaps by his Dickensian name of Mr Baulkwill), many Shavians believed that the Public Trustee had secretly been supporting the British Museum. On appeal this case had become a pretence behind which negotiations for an out-of-court settlement could take place. 'Efforts are being made to reach agreement, I understand, between certain beneficiaries under the will and the Public Trustee, who is Shaw's executor, and the Attorney-General,' reported *The Daily Telegraph* on 29 October 1957.

When 'Public Trustee v. Day and Others' came up before the Court of Appeal on 19 December, the court approved the terms of this agreement. 'My only regret,' said the Master of the Rolls, Baron Evershed (who was assisted by Lords Justice Romer and Ormerod) 'is that we are deprived of hearing what might have been very interesting arguments.' Counsel for the Public Trustee agreed: 'From a lawyer's point of view it is rather a pity.' Counsel for the Attorney-General, for the Trustees of the British Museum and the Royal Academy of Dramatic Art, for the Governors and Guardians of the National Gallery of Ireland all joined in the laughter.

*

The terms of this compromise were made public by Mr Baulkwill immediately the appeals had been dismissed. A sum of £8,300 (equivalent to £70,000 in 1990) had been entrusted to him by the residuary legatees, and he was allocating £500 of this amount as the prize in a competition for the new phonetic alfabet. The closing date was to be 1 January 1959, and he had appointed a committee of assessors to help him with the task of finding a winner: Peter MacCarthy, Head of the Department of Phonetics at the University of Leeds, Alan Dodson, chief typographer at the Stationery Office (who later resigned on going to live in South Africa), and James Pitman. The copyright of the new alfabet would be vested in the Public Trustee who would try to persuade the English-speaking world to use it. 'It will take any intelligent person only twenty-four hours to learn it with slow progress,' James Pitman predicted.

With an army of 50,000 transliterated copies of *Androcles*, Pitman believed the new model alfabet would prove invincible. But to Barbara Smoker's mind £8,300 was a 'paltry sum' which might possibly fund a bi-alphabetic *Androcles* but could never promote the vital statistical survey into phonetic economy. In seizing the shadow of Shaw's idea, might they not be losing something of substance? 'The three residuary legatees may confidently expect to share more than a hundred times the alphabet allocation,' she complained; 'so they have hardly strained the quality of mercy in favour of a cause which their benefactor had at heart.'

She too had this cause at heart. But she could not carry her complaints too far without appearing churlish to James Pitman. It was he who had negotiated the £8,300 and without him the poor alfabet might have received nothing at all. Alternatively it might have been awarded

£15,000 or won the appeal. Once more they disagreed, once again they sank these disagreements in their adjoining passion. They wanted to free the association between ideas and signs from common conventions. For the subject held a compelling beauty for them. They knew the public was deaf to these harmonious symbols and their reverberating possibilities. They knew that they might be classed with idiots who 'scribbled obscene pencillings in public lavatories'. Nevertheless, like the person who invented zero in the numerical system and gave rise to dreams of riches, they shared a common purpose of lifting this alphabetic burden, carved in stone in the dim ages, from the human mind. In their differing styles, they dreamed of replacing man's antiquated utensils and unearthing the clue to a mystery: why was it that spoken communication had always been comparatively rapid, easy and delightful, and written communication cumbrous and wearisome? Was there a deficiency in the optic nerve, a superiority in the aural nerve? This was a fundamental question on which the continuation of our literary tradition might depend. 'Why do we use a long series of arbitrary marks to represent what the voice utters at a single effort?' Sir Isaac Pitman had asked in his *Introduction to Phonography*. 'Why, in short, are not our *written signs* as simple as *spoken sounds*?' Shaw had reminded James Pitman of his grandfather's words when inviting him to keep a friendly eye on the progress of his will. To carry through the alphabetical clauses in this will, 'which generously and ingeniously sought to achieve for the language he so greatly loved the dearly cherished hopes of an exceptional man', was now James Pitman's sacramental mission.

My Fair Lady began its record-breaking run at London's Drury Lane Theatre in the spring of 1958. By the autumn James Pitman had inserted a two-page advertisement of the proposed alfabet into the programme sponsored by the silversmiths Mappin & Webb. Many of Shaw's ideas 'were so novel and penetrating that they were rejected by his contemporaries', he wrote, '– and this particular idea was so novel, and so demanding in its need to think freshly, that very few people have yet understood it'. He requested members of the audience to 'keep a space in your bookshelf' for the bi-alphabetic *Androcles*. Designs for the new alfabet were coming in from all parts of the world, and when eventually it was established we could look forward to savings in paper, ink, machine-time, storage and transport 'of £3,000,000 or $10,000,000 *a day*'.

By the end of 1958, four hundred and sixty-seven valid entries for the contest had been received by the Public Trustee. More than half of them came from the United Kingdom, but there were sixty from the United States, forty from Canada, eleven from India, ten from Germany, six from Ireland and several from Africa, South America and Eastern Europe. 'We were astonished by the merit and quantity of the work produced,' remarked James Pitman a year later. It had taken him and Peter MacCarthy the whole of 1959 to find a winner and even then they had failed to do so, coming up instead with four 'semi-winners'. Dr S. L. Pugmire, a psychiatrist working with mentally handicapped children at the Whittingham Hospital near Preston, had produced a geometric design; Mr Kingsley Read, the author of *Quickscript*, who had designed everything from pavilions for trade fairs to suits of armour for pageants and had corresponded with G.B.S. in the 1940s, submitted a cursive system; and there were script or 'current' alphabets from Mrs Pauline Bassett from Nova Scotia and Mr J. F. Magrath, an insurance broker, who had worked out his design on daily train journeys between London and Kent. All of them received cheques for £125 and the Public Trustee announced that the four winning alphabets would be co-ordinated to produce a final design for use in implementing Shaw's wishes. 'We are launching a ship,' declared Mr Baulkwill, 'and we don't know where it's going.'

It did not look to Barbara Smoker as if this vessel would get far. She regretted Shaw's failure to tie up his trusts with infant literacy. Had he nominated Enid Blyton's *Noddy* instead of his own *Androcles* the Chancery Court decision would have 'undoubtedly gone the other way'. She also deplored the absence of any expert calligrapher or educational psychologist among the assessors, and pointed out that any fusion between the four winning designs was impossible. James Pitman however felt exuberant. The final alfabet was an improved version of Kingsley Read's aesthetically pleasing forty-eight letter 'sound-writing' system. It contained little reference to the other three versions but was 'better than most other alphabets', conceded Barbara Smoker who was to be employed as specialist editor on the new *Androcles*.

In February 1961 *The Times* announced that this special edition of *Androcles* 'is likely to be on the bookstalls by early autumn'. By December the Public Trustee, who had now been knighted, forecast publication early in the New Year. On 26 February the *Daily Mail* unveiled a scoop:

'The secret publishers of the weird, phonetic version of *Androcles and the Lion* which George Bernard Shaw provided for in his will, have been unmasked.

'And it turns out that this is another scoop for Sir Allen Lane and his Penguins, who published *Lady Chatterley's Lover*, the money-spinner of 1961.'

The delay had been largely caused by contradictory instructions from Pitman, Penguin, the expert Phonetician and the Public Trustee, Sir Reginald Baulkwill. Eventually Barbara Smoker 'walked out in a huff' leaving Hans Schmoller, the publisher's renowned master of typography, floundering among the hieroglyphics of 'the world's strangest typeface'.

Androcles and the Lion, An Old Fable Renovated by Bernard Shaw with a Parallel Text in Shaw's Alphabet to be Read in Conjunction Showing its Economies in Writing and Reading was finally published on 22 November 1962. The Public Trustee's issue comprised 13,000 copies of which 12,680 were presented free to libraries: 1,900 within the United Kingdom, 1,230 around the Commonwealth, 8,690 to the United States, 710 to Canada and throughout South America and 150 to 'National Libraries of the World'. Approximately 34,000 copies of an ordinary issue costing 3s 6d were on sale to the public, an indeterminate number being exported to the United States from the second English impression. Within each copy a white Guide Card was inserted on which two keys to the alphabet (one arranged phonetically for writers, the other graphically for readers) were duplicated from the last pages of the book. There were also some 'Suggestions for Writing' supplied by Kingsley Read, some 'Notes on the Spelling' from Peter MacCarthy and a Foreword by the new Public Trustee, C. R. Sopwith (Sir Reginald Baulkwill having retired to Devon). The book was dedicated to James Pitman, now Sir James Pitman KBE, 'in grateful acknowledgement of his unstinted cooperation and continuous support over a period of nine years in carrying out Bernard Shaw's wishes'.

It was a kind of triumph. The poetry lay in its algebra and arithmetic, and in the mysterious dream encoded by these symbols and ciphers. In a disarming Introduction James Pitman sought to advise readers on the choreography of its use. 'Open the book and hold it upside down in front of a mirror,' he counselled. '... Keep the back of the book pressed against your lips, and advance towards the mirror until you are able to see individual characters clearly enough to be able to copy them.' Before long, he promised, users would be able to speed up such exercises and for those who attained gymnastic facility 'reading may be 50–75 per cent, and writing 80–100 per cent faster, and even 200–300 per cent, by using simple abbreviations'. He urged owners of this wonderful book to make their friends buy copies so that they could all correspond with one another in the new script. The following year he offered to form circles of five or six of these correspondents who, 'drawn together in a friendship by Shaw's alphabet, will all circulate their own letters to which each in turn will add'. But the success was more experimental than popular, and Pitman remained puzzled as to why these dancing circles never joined and multiplied as he hoped. He was disappointed too by the conservatism of the Ministry of Education which was offered Shaw's alfabet in principle, in draft and upon completion, and turned it down at all three stages. But Shaw's trusts did assist in the temporary success of Pitman's Initial Teaching Alphabet for children, and encouraged him to go on and on battering at the walls of prejudice until his death in 1985.

Barbara Smoker still campaigns. From time to time, when not producing strings of verse with which to tie up the deity, conducting gay and lesbian weddings, speaking from the public gallery of the House of Commons against the Vietnam War or, an elderly lady now, being knocked to the ground with her Free Speech banner by crowds of Muslims calling for the death of Salman Rushdie, she has returned to her alphabetic high ground to see if the walls have yet come tumbling down. 'History is certainly on the side of a new alphabet,' she believes. '. . . It is absurd that in the twentieth century we should still be using what is basically the ancient Phoenician alphabet, with its cumbersome letters and its bad phonetics . . . If Shaw's dream comes true – a dream shared by men of vision for nearly five centuries – who knows what miracles of human progress it may bring in its wake?'

The interest in Shaw's alfabet rose with the renovated *Androcles* and then waned. There were few funds left for the clinical survey. Peter MacCarthy handed this over to one of his students, Gordon Walsh, who went off to conduct his investigations from the University of Ife in Nigeria. The first part of his paper was completed in September 1967. But since 'Shavian is not available in Nigeria', Gordon Walsh concluded, it was 'necessary for tests to be conducted in Britain'. A year later *The Times* announced that the report was finished and that there would 'shortly be an exploratory meeting' to discuss whether it should be published. In January 1970 *The Scotsman* revealed that the results would soon be made known. 'If my report had been dramatic or epoch-making,' volunteered Peter MacCarthy, 'it would have been doubtless published before.' When questioned about the findings in March 1970, the Public Trustee, Mr Brian Davies (Sir Charles Sopwith having gone to the Inland Revenue), replied: 'It's not very urgent, and I'm very busy.' Though he had forecast early publication, he privately believed that publication was impossible. There was no more money (equivalent to nothing in 1990) for tests to be conducted in Britain. The impression of a full report was conveyed, and an appearance of publication presented sometime in the 1970s. The conclusions 'hardly caused a ripple of public interest', Barabara Smoker vaguely recalled. In any event, as Peter MacCarthy made plain, all that had been attempted was the technical discharge of the Public Trustee's obligations. Sometimes he wondered if it had all been a Shavian joke.

2

Why not a Financial Symphony?
Shaw to Elgar (29 June 1932)

In the spirit of the new age, public interest quickly veered off from the letters to the figures, following the trail of money to the three residuary legatees. There had been rumours that Shaw's bequest to the British Museum was enabling the government to cut back its normal subsidy. 'I impress upon the Financial Secretary that the last thing Bernard Shaw would have wished was to relieve the Treasury,' said the Labour Member of Parliament Emrys Hughes. Sir Edward Boyle, Financial Secretary to the Treasury, assured the House that G.B.S.'s literary work had not been financing an armaments programme. When reminded by James Pitman that Shaw's bequest to the trustees of the British Museum had been 'in acknowledgment of the incalculable value to me of my daily resort to the Reading Room of that Institution', Sir Edward Boyle revealed that over the two years money had been coming in from Shaw's royalties, £163,924 had been received by the museum, and up to £85,000 was owing to it in repayments of tax levied on the income of the estate prior to the settlement of the court action (the total equivalent to £2,000,000 in 1990). The terms of the bequest were legally 'unrestricted' in the sense that the trustees of the museum were free to do what they liked with this money and all further income over the next forty years. But since the income would virtually cease after the year 2000, when the main copyrights lapsed, a capital fund had been set up. And so that 'no act of discourtesy was done to the dead', explained Sir Edward Boyle, the trustees of the British Museum had decided that income from this capital sum 'should in due course be used primarily for the benefit of the library'.

Two years later the museum's assistant secretary reported that most of the money received had been invested by a firm of merchant bankers 'on the best terms the market will offer'. In answer to a question from the Fabian Member of Parliament John Parker, a Vice President of the Shaw Society, the Under-Secretary of State at the Department of Education and Science, Jennie Lee (later Baroness Lee of Asheridge), stated that £646,417-4s-3d (equivalent to £4,000,000 in 1990) had come to the British Museum as its share in Bernard Shaw's estate by the end of 1965.

'Sir David Wilson and the trustees are to be congratulated on the funds they have raised to improve the display of the collections,' wrote Lord Annan in 1991. During the previous fifteen years the royalty income of the Shaw Estate had settled down to between £275,000 and £500,000 a year. 'I conclude that in the fullness of time the whole library department of the Museum will benefit,' a *Sunday Times* journalist had predicted. But when the library department separated from the museum in 1973, no reference was officially made to a Shaw capital fund to be used 'primarily for the benefit of the library'.

Donations from the Shaw Fund towards heritage purchases by the British Museum Manuscripts Department and the British Library between 1960 and 1990 amounted to approximately £400,000 – or a little over £13,000 a year on average. Such donations were given as 'a matter of grace' on the part of the British Museum Trustees, and since the British Library executive was never shown the accounts of the Trust it could not know how small a proportion of the Shaw Fund's expenditure it received – less than one tenth of its growing income. So the very 'act of discourtesy . . . to the dead' that Sir Edward Boyle assured the House of Commons in 1959 would not be committed actually was committed. In an attempt to clarify matters, the Shadow Minister for the Arts, Mark Fisher, asked some questions similar to those put by James Pitman and John Parker in the House of Commons in 1959 and 1965: what in effect was the total sum that had accrued to the British Museum by the end of 1990 and what was properly due to the British Library? But the Minister with responsibility for Arts and Libraries, Tim Renton, answered that this was 'not a subject on which I have any specific responsibility'. On the advice of the Director of the British Museum, Sir David Wilson, the Trustees had decided not to disclose the figure to anyone because they were 'the Trustees' private monies' and public disclosure would enable Treasury officials to take the Shaw income into account when determining the British Museum's annual grant. The annual amounts from the Shaw bequest were audited by the Comptroller and Auditor-General, but expenditure was not scrutinized by the Public Accounts Committee or the Treasury.

It was open for Sir David Wilson and his trustees to transfer this problem on to the shoulders of the British Library, along with the money Shaw had plainly intended to be used for library purposes. But short of such an act of integrity, the British Museum's secrecy seemed pragmatic in view of what happened to another of Shaw's residuary legatees, the Royal Academy of Dramatic Art.

*

Shaw had been fond of RADA. He gave lectures to its students, campaigned for the introduction of women to its governing body, served as a member of its council from 1911 to 1941 (coming to 102 of its 141 meetings in that period), and contributed £5,000 towards its new building in Gower Street in the 1920s (equivalent to £100,000 in 1990). His bequest, which was to change the status of the Academy, brought about a crisis in the summer of 1965. 'Is My Fair Lady behind the real-life drama at RADA?' queried *The Sunday Times*. On 30 May that year the Academy's Principal, John Fernald, suddenly resigned. Fernald had been on the teaching staff at RADA before the war, then in the late 1940s became director of the Liverpool Playhouse before being appointed Principal of RADA in 1955. As a director he possessed a controlled lightness of touch and a quality of lyricism that worked especially well with Chekhov. He was well liked by the RADA students, the more impecunious of whom he would help out with gifts of money for travel, lodging and food. He soon raised the standards of teaching by weeding out frivolous applications from rich débutantes, arranging student tours round the country and overseas, and widening the experience of his young trainees by bringing back talented ex-students to act with them. A few big decisions, such as the building of an expensive new rehearsal room, were taken in Council. But for the most part he and his bursar, Sybil Topham, liked to settle everything between them. After all, most things were fundamentally simple. He regarded the Shaw money 'as a means of helping his students, whom he adored,' remembered his daughter Karin Fernald.

By the mid-1960s the Academy had accumulated a capital of £750,000 (equivalent to more than £5,000,000 in 1990) and the Shaw bequest was producing a yearly income exceeding £30,000 (over £200,000 in 1990). This fortune, which transformed RADA from an orphan to an heiress, awakened interest among the governing body, in particular the film producer Sir Michael Balcon. At that time the administration as well as the artistic direction was vested in the Principal. But Fernald took little interest in administration. He kept no proper accounting system and had failed to maximize the benefits of Shaw's royalties with a professional investment policy. To the rising financial men he appeared guileless, and they questioned the validity of his costly tours for students.

This was a watershed in the Academy's affairs as it moved from the gentle ebb and flow of the amateur world towards the boom and crash of modern marketing. At an extraordinary general meeting held on the morning of Tuesday 13 July 1965 and crowded with famous actors, what some newspapers called 'the Battle of Gower Street' was fought out between Fernald's loyal supporters led by Richard Briers and Peter O'Toole and the governing body led by Sir Felix Aylmer. Both Fernald and Aylmer were Vice-Presidents of the Shaw Society, a stage-direction which gave Shavian piquancy to the contest.

This backstage drama erupted into the newspapers after RADA turned down an offer from John Fernald to withdraw his resignation. An army of actors paraded through the streets calling on the governing body itself to resign. Then the Privy Council met to investigate technical misdemeanours and, following changes to the Academy's charter, new elections were held. There was a fresh splash of discord and further ripples of publicity: then an Administrator-Registrar was appointed and a Finance Office created 'to allow the Principal to concentrate on training and the educational side of things'. But this did not impress John Fernald who believed that 'the constraints imposed by a non-artistic administrator have usually been found to be at the best unacceptable, and at the worst, unworkable'. He left England to run another drama school and theatre in Michigan in the United States, and during the 1970s took a professorial post in the Department of Theater at New York State University.

Over the years, while RADA's accounts continued to show a deficit, the springs of Shaw's bequest revived a three-year Acting Diploma course as well as two-year Stage Management and Specialist Technical courses. The money was also used to buy new equipment and top up the maintenance of students relying on a declining system of discretionary awards.

Then, early in 1990, though still based in Gower Street (which it leased from the University of London), the Academy purchased the freehold of a building nearby at 18 Chenies Street. The cost was £5,250,000. It was financed by a government grant of £500,000, a donation of £1,000,000 from British Telecom, and the sale of shares worth £3,750,000 from the RADA portfolio largely made up from Shaw's invested royalties. This was supplemented late in 1991 by a grant of £500,000 from the Foundation for Sport and the Arts for conversion costs. In 1962 the Academy had become an independent charity and the acquisition of these new premises was intended as a further step towards the ideal of self-sufficiency when Shaw's royalties cease after the year 2000.

Would the Academy have been able to achieve more, become self-supporting, with more government aid? Or would it have subsided into aid-dependency? Would it have survived at all without Shaw's money? The chairman, Sir Richard Attenborough, believes it must have closed. During the Thatcher decade there was no choice for arts organizations but to expel the dilettante and measure efficiency by profit. But some of the dangers of implementing arts-marketing without the introduction of new tax laws had been spelt out a quarter of a century earlier when James Pitman argued in Parliament in favour of special arrangements for legacies to public and charitable institutions wholly or partly supported by government funds. If the Exchequer contribution to such institutions was consequently reduced, he explained, the purpose of the testator would be rendered void to the detriment of the public's future interests.

In the case of Shaw's estate, the Exchequer had already imposed death duties of more than £500,000 in the 1950s. Shaw's intention was not to benefit to any greater extent the generality of taxpayers but to favour two special sections of the public: those who would be using 'the Reading Room of the British Museum and those would-be actors, actresses and producers who would be thus receiving better training themselves for a part in the dramatic arts'. The Financial Secretary to the Treasury, Sir Edward Boyle (later Baron Boyle of Handsworth), had assured the House of Commons in December 1959 that the Treasury objected strongly to the principle that trustees should use trust funds 'in a way which would merely reduce their demand on public funds, either to maintain an existing service or to start a new one'.

'The Treasury even in times of great stringency in our national and economic affairs has never sought to argue that the cost of a service should be reduced by a contribution from other resources available to the Trustees, or that public funds should not be provided to improve a service merely because the Trustees could afford to do it themselves . . . I do not think there has been a convenient occasion for stating the principle, which I think is an important one, that in deciding the expenditure on Vote-borne departments we do not say that the Treasury contribution should be automatically reduced simply because some other source may become available.'

Between principle and practice, private and public money, swirled many confusing cross-currents. In 1967, less than two years after John Fernald's resignation and the fall-out of publicity over Shaw's bequest, the Treasury cancelled its grant to RADA. This lesson was not lost on its co-residuary legatee, the British Museum. Until the mid-1960s the trustees had been happy to make known what money was accruing to the museum from Shaw's royalties and to explain how it was primarily to be used. But over the next twenty-five years, as the cumulative underfunding of national arts institutions grew worse, secrecy and guile seemed to be forced upon those trying to represent the best interests of these institutions. Every one of them was in competition with every other one for sponsorship and grants, even complementary bodies such as the British Museum and British Library. It was not difficult in such embattled circumstances to overlook the wishes of the dead.

What were Shaw's wishes? When he referred to the British Museum in his letters, the context shows that he had in mind the library or manuscripts department of the museum (later the British Library Reference Division). 'Why do you not get a reader's ticket at the British Museum,' he asks his Polish translator Floryan Sobieniowski. 'I spent every day of my life there for several years.' His debt to that great institution 'contracted in the early days when I read and worked for many years in its Reading Room,' he explained to Edy Craig, 'is inestimable, and gives it a right to anything of mine that is of sufficient public interest to be worthy of its acceptance.' What he described in his will as 'such

letters and documents as might be worth preserving in a public collection such as that of the British Museum,' including the drafts of eighteen
plays, were handed to the Manuscripts Department by the Public Trustee and now form the centre of its large Shaw Collection.

'There are people in this country who are watching very closely the
interests of Bernard Shaw ... to see that the purpose for which [he] left
his money will be fulfilled,' Emrys Hughes had told Parliament at the
end of the 1950s. But as such people died, the knowledge of these
interests and that purpose faded. This was what James Pitman had
warned the House of Commons might happen. 'Let it not be said in the
world of literature and throughout the whole English-speaking world,'
he exhorted his fellow Members of Parliament, 'that a great Irishman
and genius of the English language who sought to help English literature
and English drama found honourable respect for the terms of his will
only in Ireland.'

*

Compared with its English counterparts the National Gallery of Ireland
had what *The Sunday Times* described in the early 1960s as a 'delightful'
policy 'which is to invest not in shares but in pictures'. No tablets were
then placed under pictures bought by the gallery showing the source of
the purchase money, and there was no list of the works bought from the
Shaw Fund. Gradually rumours began circulating in Dublin pubs that
Shaw's money had been spent on a number of marvellous fakes and
forgeries. Barbara Smoker, arriving from London in the 1960s and
asking to see some pictures bought from the Shaw bequest, was shown a
couple of religious works by Murillo and a Crucifix by Giovanni di Paolo
(a rare and highly valued work) which considerably offended her.
Twenty years later, when challenged to put on an exhibition of selected
works bought from the Shaw Fund over a quarter of a century so as to
celebrate the old patronage and invite new business sponsorship, the
director of the gallery regretfully declined because 'it will not be within
our resources to mount the Shaw show'. The gallery's resources were
shortly afterwards reported in the *Sunday Press*. According to figures
supplied to the Comptroller and Auditor-General, £164,714 had been
received by the gallery from the Shaw bequest in the twelve months
ending on 31 March 1990, and the total in investments and at the bank
was £751,173. This sum attracted the notice of the Shaw Birthplace
Trust which, with a £60,000 overdraft, had bought 33 Synge Street the

previous year for £111,000 and was endeavouring to create a Shaw museum in the near-derelict building. Threatened with an appeal from this Trust, the director of the National Gallery, Raymond Keaveney, replied that 'We have had our own contingencies since then and the sum in the Shaw bequest is very much smaller.'

The 'delightful policy' of simply buying pictures had long been modified by the Governors and Guardians of the gallery. Increasingly money from the Shaw Fund was spent on the insurance of paintings and, in the 1980s, on the conversion and refurbishment of an extension to the gallery at 90 Merrion Square, as well as on the purchase of other sites in Clare Street and Clare Lane. The last work bought by the gallery was a modest, rather indifferent picture by William Ashford called *A bowl of flowers* in 1985.

The gallery's stewardship of the Shaw bequest during much of the thirty-three years it has been receiving Shaw's royalties has been set out by one of the Keepers, Dr Michael Wynne.

'As monies come in from the royalties we endeavour to allow the substantial sum to be accumulated, and from this we buy significant works of art and designate that they have been purchased from the George Bernard Shaw Fund. Occasionally some of the works bought from the fund are relatively minor. This situation arises when towards the end of the financial year we have spent all the government grant for acquisitions and are anxious to seize the opportunity of acquiring something that is important for the collection.'

What was important for the collection was the strengthening of various schools of painting. This has meant that the Shaw Fund purchases were not artistically integral and could not be made to 'form an exhibition of a worthiness due to our great benefactor', Dr Wynne explains (though a very interesting exhibition of this sort was shown in 1987 from purchases made by Sir Michael Levey on his retirement as Director of the National Gallery in London). Nearer the year 2000, Dr Wynne believes, it may be appropriate to publish a brochure with illustrations in colour and a comprehensive list of Shaw acquisitions. 'In the meantime the best tribute which we can pay is to make sure that the purchases made through the Shaw Fund are correctly labelled, and have the descriptions of them published through books like your own.' In 1991 Dr Wynne compiled a list of these purchases from the gallery records (see Appendix C).

The outstanding features of the gallery's collection have been a small but spectacularly good choice of seventeenth-century French paintings (among which are an excellent Claude and Poussin), special attention to religious art which has resulted in a fine holding of Italian Baroque pictures, and some creditable examples of Irish art. The list of works bought from the Shaw Fund shows how the gallery has complemented these areas with a number of art-historically interesting pictures. To the Claude and Poussin, for example, it has added a composition by a comparatively rare painter Louis Le Nain, a late and beautiful Vouet (whose reputation following an exhibition in Paris early in 1991 has been rapidly rising) and a fascinating work (*The Image of Saint Alexis*) showing the extraordinary effects of light by Etienne de la Tour, son of the more famous Georges de la Tour. Additions to the eighteenth-century collection include a rather dull Nattier, but also an excellent portrait by the Swedish painter (of the French school) Roslin and, merging into the nineteenth century, an early and uncommon Baroque studio work, David's *Funeral of Patroclus*. A more characteristic example of David's school is represented by the portrait of Marie-Julie Bonaparte by his pupil Baron Gérard.

The Italian Baroque section at the gallery, which has works by artists such as Castiglione, Lorenzo Lippi, Felice Ficherelli and Carlo Dolci who are little represented in the United Kingdom and were bought cheap earlier in the century when religious pictures were not greatly valued elsewhere, has been enriched by a unique battle scene from Tasso by Cigoli, a major seventeenth-century Florentine painter. The two Murillos (one characteristic, the other untypical) were presumably bought to add to the Roman Catholic content of the collection. Unable to afford a Simone Martini, the gallery bought instead *The Annunciation* painted in 1410 by Jacques Iverny. It cost £250,000 in 1965 and is valued at considerably more than ten times that sum twenty-five years later. The gallery also picked up a wrongly attributed painting of a sleeping girl, a subtle exploration of virtually one colour, later confirmed as a Goya.

The plan appears to have been to buy Renaissance and Baroque sculpture in the 1960s and 1970s when, as compared with Old Master paintings, this sculpture was inexpensive. The two works by Richier, the sixteenth-century French Renaissance sculptor, are remarkable purchases, Duquesnoy's *Cardinal Guido Bentivoglio* is the bust of a distinguished art patron (who discovered Claude Lorrain) by a comparatively unknown yet impressive sculptor.

The Irish school has been reinforced with some eighteenth- and early nineteenth-century landscapes, notably two beautiful paintings by Nathaniel Grogan, three pictures by the idiosyncratic Jack Yeats and Nathaniel Hone's satire on Reynolds as an eclectic artist, a masterpiece which provides a commentary on eighteenth-century art theory and, possibly better than any other single work, conveys the spirit of these Shaw Fund purchases.

Perhaps there is the odd picture from which Shaw himself would have recoiled (though his art criticism does not reveal him as being irredeemably hostile to religious paintings). He would see, however, that the collection he had got to know as a boy as he wandered through the gallery rooms, catching sight of a larger imaginative world and dreaming of being an artist himself, has been greatly enhanced through his bequest.

*

Two further threads appear in the financial tapestry of Shaw's estate. When his seagoing uncle, the Rabelaisian doctor Walter John Gurly, had died at the end of the nineteenth century, G.B.S. found himself the owner of 'his cursed property and debts' in Carlow. He had little power to control or direct the management of these Irish properties, and instead of title deeds had received a bundle of mortgages and a packet of worthless pawn tickets. 'A horrible misfortune has happened to me – a money trouble,' he notified Ellen Terry a few days after coming into his inheritance.

'I have succeeded through the death of my uncle to a family estate in Ireland – a miserable relic of former country splendour, all mortgages and poor relations ... My blessed uncle had not paid even his servant's wages for ten years, and had borrowed every farthing he could. I shall have to pay his debts because I am inheriting the privileges of paying the interest on half a dozen Carlow mortgages.'

The principal site was known as the Old Assembly Rooms in the centre of Carlow. It was a fair-sized building, measuring some ninety feet in depth and commanding a fifty-foot frontage described by the *Carlow Nationalist* as being 'inspiringly designed in the style of the classic revival of the eighteenth century, characteristic of Irish Public buildings of that date'. For many years it functioned as some class of a country club and was used for public entertainments, though according to Shaw's uncle it would have made a better observatory as you 'could watch the movements of the heavenly bodies through the holes in the roof'.

In 1915 Shaw received a petition inviting him to present this property to the town of Carlow for use as a technical school. 'At present,' he was told, 'the classes in Technical Instruction are being held in makeshift premises. Consequently instruction is very much restricted.' As the consideration for this deal he was promised that his 'honoured name will be revered in perpetuity'.

These Assembly Rooms had long been a bad bargain for G.B.S., costing him over the years almost three hundred pounds. He had hesitated between allowing himself to be evicted by stopping payment of the head rents and inventing a sale of the imposing façade to an American millionaire for re-erection in the United States. On the whole it seemed better to have his name 'revered in perpetuity'. Besides, from the public point of view, there was a good deal to be said for complying with this request. 'Unfortunately the place is leased and subleased,' he replied. '... Lately I had all but succeeded in buying out the lessor when he fell into the Barrow and was drowned; and I have not yet succeeded in discovering who his successor is.' It took Shaw until the autumn of 1919 finally to disencumber the Assembly Rooms and sign the deed transferring them to Carlow 'in consideration of the place being used for public purposes and (if possible) the old front of the building being retained for the sake of its decorative effect'. The property was later turned into a Vocational School and after Shaw's death, its façade still intact, has become the County Library Headquarters.

The remaining seventeen parcels of Gurly property (including a burial ground called 'The Graves') Shaw retained for another twenty-five years. 'I am myself a landlord, and, what is worse, an absentee landlord,' he wrote in *Everybody's Political What's What?* 'Since I inherited my property ... I once spent a few hours in its neighborhood without entering or identifying a single house on it.' To assist matters he employed a local man, Major Fitzmaurice, as his business agent. 'Many people who dont know me (and perhaps some who do),' he told Fitzmaurice, 'imagine that I am a difficult man to deal with because my writings rub them up the wrong way.' Actually most of his tenants soon came to realize that he was peculiarly soft-hearted. Sometimes he would receive bills from Carlow shopkeepers due from his tenants who had pledged his credit by guaranteeing payment from him in London. 'I wonder would Mrs Aylward take £50 to leave the country and settle in China,' he wrote of one tenant who regularly calculated at the end of each quarter that he owed her money. His correspondence with Major Fitzmaurice shows him to have been forever making the roofs good, guarding against vandalism, replacing cisterns, clearing gutters. 'My attempts to repair houses on my estate have generally begun by the collapse of the whole edifice,' he admitted. By his eighty-eighth year he decided that 'if I could live another 88 years I would knock down every house on the property and replace it with a new one, with a garage and a modern kitchen, with all the latest labor saving contrivances and conditioned air, to teach the Carlovians to want such things'.

In his published writings G.B.S. represented himself as a conventional absentee landlord in order to show up the legal impropriety of the property market. 'I pocket a modest income from it, earned by the labor of its inhabitants, who have never seen me nor received any service from me,' he confessed. 'A grosser malversation can hardly be imagined; but it is not my fault: I have to accept it as the law of the land; for there is no alternative open to me. I am strongly in favor of this little estate of mine being municipalized.'

With this in mind he wrote asking the Taoiseach Éamon de Valera in May 1945 to introduce into the Dáil a new law enabling local authorities to accept, hold and administer gifts of property provided they adopt a 'Civic Improvement Scheme'. To his delight, this Local Authorities (Acceptance of Gifts) Bill was quickly drafted and passed that summer. 'Splendid!' Shaw congratulated de Valera. 'It would have taken thirty years in this unhappy country.' On 13 August 1945 all Shaw's Carlow property was passed to the Urban District Council. According to the Act, civic improvement included anything that tended to 'improve the amenities' of the area or was 'conducive to the welfare of the inhabitants'. A condition of all gifts, and their income, was that they could not be absorbed into general assets for the relief of rates since, drawing on his experience on the St Pancras Vestry, Shaw believed that a reduction in rates merely assisted landlords 'on whom the rates finally fell, without benefiting the country or improving the town'.

'I am far too good a Socialist to believe that Socialism can be established by private enterprise,' Shaw had written to Major Fitzmaurice. Yet by his own private enterprise he had established a modest instalment of socialism in Ireland. For nearly twenty-five years the Carlow Urban

District Council made financial help available from its Shaw Fund for cultural and artistic purposes. But subsequent legislation in Ireland, including the Local Government (Planning and Development) Act 1963, the Housing Act 1966, and the Arts Act 1973, all of which enabled local councils to subsidize a widening range of endeavours out of the rates, brought about a Gilbertian situation in which the Shaw Fund could not be used for any identifiable civic improvement without being in breach of its rates relief condition. For another twenty-five years, while lawyers brooded on this predicament, the funds were frozen at the bank except for one strange payment each December to erect a Christmas Crib at the Courthouse. Tiring of this stalemate, the Carlovians eventually came up with a brainwave, and invited the British ambassador to open their own Shaw-funded Shaw Festival in 1991 with its programme of lectures, workshops in the Old Assembly Rooms, school prizes, musical events (including a selection from *My Fair Lady*), the renaming of the Town Park after G.B.S. and a spirited production of *How He Lied to Her Husband*.

The last financial thread was spun from Shaw's Nobel Prize for Literature. 'I cannot persuade myself to accept the money,' he had written in November 1926 to the Royal Swedish Academy. Four months later, on 27 March 1927, he signed a Trust Deed creating an Anglo-Swedish Literary Foundation for the translation into English of classical Swedish literature. To this he donated all his prize money, which amounted to 118,165 Swedish Kronor then worth approximately £6,500 (equivalent to £130,000 in 1990).

The objects of the Anglo-Swedish Literary Foundation were defined in the Trust Deed as 'the encouragement of cultural intercourse between Sweden and the British Islands through the promotion and diffusion of knowledge and appreciation of the literature and art of Sweden in the British Islands'. The first patron of the Foundation was the King of Sweden and its trustees still include the Swedish ambassador. Though some grants were made to facilitate productions of Strindberg's plays and to support Swedish music in Britain, most of the money has been spent on the translation of Swedish books. There were translations of Swedish Nobel Prize winners Pär Lagerkvist, Eyvind Johnson and Harry Martinson, novels by Hjalmar Bergman (considered by many critics to be the greatest Swedish prose writer of the twentieth century), Strindberg's plays, anthologies of Swedish poetry and short stories, and some non-fiction including a vivid description of nineteenth-century

England by Erik Gustaf Geijer, Ingvar Andersson's history of Sweden (for many years the only history of Sweden available in English), and biographies of Carl Linnaeus by Knut Hagberg and of the Swedish composer Franz Berwald by Robert Layton.

After the Second World War the Foundation reconstructed the Swedish section in the library of University College, London, enabling it to become a centre for lending Swedish books, and made donations of books to libraries round Britain that had been depleted in the war. 'The Foundation's funds are not advertised,' wrote the Swedish cultural attaché. 'Possibly its funds are exhausted,' Shaw had written to his bibliographer Loewenstein in 1950. By 1974 its unadvertised balance at the bank appears to have dwindled alarmingly to £1,157 plus a few pence. But with a deft redefinition of its objects (replacing 'the literature and art of Sweden' with the words 'Swedish culture') the trustees were able to replenish the capital with money from the sale of the Swedish Institute's office in London.

From the early 1980s the Foundation has widened its ancillary activities by supporting the newly formed Swedish English Literary Translators' Association and its journal, *Swedish Book Review*; by assisting a translator-in-residence scheme; and enabling Swedish writers to visit Britain, English translators to visit Sweden. In 1991 this contribution to Anglo-Swedish relations from the man who was 'dead against prizes' was recognized by the creation of a three-yearly Bernard Shaw Prize. The first prize was presented at the Swedish Embassy in London to Tom Geddes for his translation of Torgny Lindgren's novel, *The Way of a Serpent*.

*

'Please do not ask Mr Bernard Shaw for money,' reads a blue-green stereotyped postcard G.B.S. had drafted in 1935. 'He has not enough to help the large number of his readers who are in urgent need of it. He can write for you: he cannot finance you.' During the last fifteen years of his life he fended off an increasing number of appellants with variously coloured cards. But though gaining a reputation for thrift, he still received a mass of appeals from 'charitable institutions, religious sects and churches, inventors, Utopian writers desirous of establishing international millennial leagues, parents unable to afford secondary education for their children: in short, everybody and every enterprise in financial straits of any sort'.

Such appeals were founded on the notion that he was a multi-millionaire whereas, he would explain, all his income 'except enough to meet his permanent engagements is confiscated by the Exchequer and redistributed to those with smaller tax-free incomes or applied to general purposes from which everyone benefits'. He did not complain of this system, 'having advocated it for half a century, and nationalized all his landed property,' but his correspondents could not have his income in cash from himself as well as in services from their country. 'It is useless to ask him for money: he has none to spare,' reads a rose-coloured card drafted in 1949. Then, having demonstrated that 'No other reply to appeals is possible,' he would secrete a cheque into his envelopes for the Actors' Orphanage, Royal Literary Fund, the Society for the Protection of Birds, the Lord Mayor's National Flood Distress Fund, the King Edward Memorial Hospital, Travellers' Aid Society, Chaim Weizmann's Zionist Appeal, the Shakespeare Memorial Theatre at Stratford-upon-Avon, the National Theatre in London and, as bail money or pension money, for eyeglasses or boots, to an always-lengthening list of individuals. 'On your life, don't tell anybody,' he warned the actor Esmé Percy, one of the most regular performer-producers of his plays, to whom he had made a gift of £100 (equivalent to £2,000 in 1990). Had he permitted such things to become public, 'his name and Charlotte's would have headed most subscription lists, for their contribution was invariably the largest'.

In his biography published in 1956, St John Ervine described Shaw's testament as being 'one of the most public-spirited documents in the whole history of bequests'. The author of *Socialism for Millionaires* (1901) became the posthumous multi-millionaire supplicants had so optimistically cherished in his lifetime. Forty years after his death his own birthplace in Synge Street lay derelict, but G.B.S. was at last becoming recognized, in the words of Dan H. Laurence, as probably 'the most charitable professional man of his generation'.

3

Great men do not, as a rule, endow their own memorials. That is for posterity...
Ivor Brown, *Time and Tide* (29 December 1951)

On the afternoon of 17 March 1951 Dame Edith Evans declared 'Shaw's Corner' open to the public. In persistent rain, like the rain that had fallen while Shaw's ashes were being scattered in the garden less than four months earlier, 200 people gathered for the ceremony at Ayot St Lawrence. Television cameras and radio microphones were there to observe and record them as they overflowed from the heated marquees on to the lawn. Invitations had been sent to everyone who knew G.B.S., from the village postmistress Jisbella Lyth to the Fabian Saint Joan Mary Hankinson. 'I knew him well and loved him, and so did my wife,' replied Sean O'Casey who was too ill to travel. 'A man of most excellent fancy. May we become more worthy of his greatness.' 'Will be in spirit with you,' Gabriel Pascal cabled from California a few days later.

Never before had the National Trust possessed a house with 'the imprint of genius still warm upon it'. Edith Evans recalled the gaiety and charm of G.B.S., his eighteenth-century manners and provocative methods of directing his own plays. 'At rehearsals he would always tell us what we did wrong,' the *News of the World* reported her as saying, 'and then act a bit to show us how to do it. I used to think his acting was terrible.'

'At one rehearsal, suddenly without any warning he bent and very swiftly kissed me. I didn't get very much pleasure out of it because I was so surprised. We all looked a bit staggered.'

The house was to be open four afternoons a week and all day on Sundays, and visitors were to be charged two shillings for admission. On Sunday 18 March some 600 of them arrived in the village and on Easter Monday there were more than 1,000. They came from all over Britain and around Europe, from Canada, South America, the United States, India, China...

'Trouble has come to Ayot,' announced the *Evening News*. Before the end of the month pandemonium was sweeping through the village. A few of the 150 inhabitants, such as the landlord of the Brocket Arms, believed they should face up to the rigours of prosperity and welcome tourists during Festival year. But most villagers were already 'fed up with being famous'. They foresaw a catastrophic future: their fields reduced to car parks, their cottages converted into cafés, their shops crammed with hideous Shavian mugs and ashtrays. Did they really want to be outnumbered ten to one by invading sightseers trampling on the flower-beds and have their way impeded by erupting litter-bins, snack-bars-on-wheels, Italianate ice-cream men in white coats? Did they want to be pointed at by screaming advertisements and deafened by the perpetual hooting of unending traffic? In short: must they live like a cursed tribe longing for the comforts of summer rain and winter snow?

These were some of the chilling questions put to villagers at an emergency meeting in the parish church. A one-armed captain stood up and ringingly declared that he would 'move heaven & earth' to get Shaw's Corner closed; a surveyor cried out that he would bring a case against the National Trust under the Town and Country Planning Act; and several younger villagers, forming themselves into guerrilla groups, set out on raiding parties and uprooted more than thirty Automobile Association signposts.

Then suddenly the trouble lifted. Fifteen thousand people came to Shaw's Corner during the first five months, but by September the figure had settled down to fewer than 2,000 a month. The police withdrew, the special bus service was discontinued, and a gentler convoy of cars and charabancs parked comfortably in what had once been Shaw's kitchen garden.

Many Shavians expected Shaw's 'friend and factotum' Dr Fritz Loewenstein to be appointed as first curator of the house. He expected it himself and had been assiduously campaigning for this appointment ever since Shaw gave his house to the National Trust in 1944. 'I beg to offer you my services,' he had written that year. ' . . . Once the National Trust has taken over the property and has come to a decision with regard to the intended Shaw Museum, you might find it desirable to have the help of somebody who is not wholly uninformed with regard to Mr Shaw's works etc., and who at the same time is an ardent admirer of the G.O.M. and all he stands for.'

While assuring him that it would be 'only too glad to enlist your help and guidance', the National Trust cautioned Loewenstein against giving Shaw the impression 'that we were discussing any future plans about his house behind his back'. This agreed, discussions continued and by the end of 1944 Loewenstein persuaded James Lees-Milne at the Trust to try out a new plan on G.B.S. This was to plant his seedling Shaw Society at Ayot St Lawrence once Shaw himself had made room for it by dying. Under Loewenstein's care the Society could then flower and Shaw's Corner come into its own as 'a meeting place for Shavians from all parts of the world, a centre for Shavian thought, a place for recreation (open air performances in the grounds) and of study' where scholars could browse on Loewenstein's rich pasture of 'old rubbish' as G.B.S. had called it. In his enthusiasm Loewenstein believed they could start making an inventory of the contents in Shaw's Corner right away. From the National Trust's offices in London he hurried down to Ayot St Lawrence and arrived in time to see G.B.S. opening this letter. 'He read it attentively but made no comment,' Loewenstein reported back. 'You will probably hear from him shortly. Kindly keep me posted.'

Shaw's letter five days later reminded the National Trust that he was also leaving it the contents of his home. He could not make an inventory of these contents because he wished to transfer 'a lot of things from London, and get rid of some superfluities'. If anything went wrong, the Trust could let the house furnished 'for £300 a year or thereabouts'. As for the Shaw Societies, they 'will all die of old age in four years at most', he added.

G.B.S. was then in his eighty-ninth year. His letter stirred some feelings of compunction in James Lees-Milne. 'I have been rather a nuisance to you, I am afraid,' he wrote. By the same post he also told Loewenstein: 'I do not feel inclined to write to him any further on the matter, as I am sure you will agree.'

Loewenstein declared himself 'delighted with Shaw's answer'. All the same, he could not altogether let the matter go no further, and over the next five years occasionally pressed the National Trust for some legal assurance over the housing of his Shaw Society. To top up the goodwill he also sent in bulletins on Shaw's health, and notes about precious objects in the house (the Rodin bust, the Augustus John portrait) for the proposed inventory. Finally, in the morning of 2 November 1950, he telephoned the National Trust's head office with news of Shaw's death and asked for a draft contract on the house.

Legally Shaw's Corner could not be 'vested' with the National Trust until probate had been granted. This gave the Trust some two and a half months in which to sort out an embarrassing financial problem. For as

Shaw's vigilant secretary Blanche Patch assured everyone, 'owing to its inaccessibility, visitors' fees would not pay for its upkeep'.

Shaw himself had originally considered his neighbours, Stephen and Clare Winsten, biographer and artist, as paying custodians. 'I have in mind a gentleman who will probably be my acting literary executor,' he had informed the Trust. 'He and his wife are very anxious to reside in the house and shew it off to visitors. They are ardent Shavians and can afford the tenancy ... ' But the Winstens had grown impatient, quarrelled with Shaw, and moved to Oxford from where they now wrote to the Trust claiming several items in the house as their own. They did not appear likely candidates for the new tenancy – besides, it 'would raise a local outcry,' Blanche Patch volunteered, 'as when they lived nearby these people never paid their bills'.

Blanche Patch was a loquacious source of information to the National Trust. For years she had been waiting to pour out her scandal into the right ears. Now she poured with a vengeance. She was especially eager to damage Loewenstein's reputation. After all, he had been nothing more than an office boy, she said, and was certainly never invited to dinner at the house. Indeed, the housekeeper Mrs Laden would not even let him sit down there for fear he would 'dirty her chairs'. Charlotte Shaw, she remembered, had also 'detested' him. It was bad enough to hear that the Public Trustee was allowing him to carry on work five days a week using Charlotte's old bedroom as his study. To give him the whole house would be sacrilege.

The National Trust's secretary Jack Rathbone could see that Miss Patch was 'plainly very jealous' of Loewenstein. But she was so full of amusing stories he could not help liking her. When he asked her whom she would recommend as curator, however, she came up with an ex-policeman from the village – a strange choice as National Trust custodian of literature.

Despite all that Blanche Patch could bring against him, Loewenstein retained strong claims on Shaw's Corner. For although the National Trust never gave him a binding undertaking, he had been led to understand that 'it would be a very satisfactory and appropriate solution for the Trust to let the building to the Shavian Society, provided we could come to terms on a financial basis particularly ... ' To meet such terms, Loewenstein now introduced a colleague who was prepared to pay the Trust £500 a year (equivalent to more than £6,000 in 1990) for a full repairing lease on the house. He proposed that the two of them occupy the top floors (part of which would also be used as an office for the Shaw Society) and maintain the three main reception rooms and the garden as a 'Shavian Shrine' for National Trust visitors. 'With due diffidence,' he wrote, 'I submit that no person or group of persons can present a better claim to tenant Shaw's lease or give a better guarantee that the property and its contents will be preserved for the benefit of the Nation as a worthy memorial.'

It was hardly surprising if Loewenstein took it for granted that he would be offered a joint tenancy. He had done everything asked of him – indeed he had done rather more, collecting extravagant messages from Shaw Societies round the world applauding the prospect of this glorious installation. But there were rumours that Lady Astor had opposed him. 'I thought for a moment of asking Lady Astor what she thought of Loewenstein,' Harold Nicolson, a National Trust vice-chairman (later Sir Harold Nicolson), wrote to the Trust's Secretary Jack Rathbone, 'but no sooner had the thought raised its little head than it popped down again. Nancy's opinion on any matter is really of little value to anybody.'

What was of value were the opinions of the arbiters and aesthetes of the National Trust itself – and these opinions were unanimous. 'We disliked Loewenstein ... intensely.' By the end of 1951 the Trust had decided that 'the Shaw Society and Dr Loewenstein should not be made responsible for the maintenance of the house unless absolutely necessary'.

It was never made clear what was so peculiarly odious about Loewenstein that he 'would be a discredit to the Trust'. Perhaps it was the fact that he was never to be seen, even for a cup of tea, without his solicitor. Or that he had, according to a fellow bibliographer, 'a servility and unction that Uriah Heep might have envied'. The fact that he was Jewish counted against him not at all, or hardly at all, not greatly anyway. It was simply that a German Jew with a foreign doctorate on Japanese prints was unlikely to understand the sophisticated operations of English life with its nuances of social elevation, its protected areas of financial accumulation. Sensing that things might not after all be going his way, he summoned the Past-Presidents and Vice-Presidents, officers and founder-members of the Shaw Society to do battle for him, men like Gabriel Pascal and Shaw's German translator Siegfried Trebitsch, the Marxist-Leninist lawyer D. N. Pritt, the American mathematician and biographer Archibald Henderson. The Trust sifted through such names and found two, the Labour Member of Parliament David Hardman and the playwright Benn Levy, whom it thought possible to approach, but neither of them would give references testifying to Loewenstein's financial respectability. 'If we could afford it,' Jack Rathbone informed Lord Crawford (alias Lord Bathniel, Baron Wigan and the eleventh Earl of Balcarres), 'I would like to keep on Mrs Laden and I think she would keep the house beautifully, and shew it well.'

Alice Laden had been Shaw's housekeeper since Charlotte's death in 1943. She dazzled everyone. 'She is an interesting-looking and obviously very efficient woman,' Jack Rathbone enthused, 'scarlet-nailed and heavily made up.' To him and Harold Nicolson and the Trust's adviser on historic buildings, James Lees-Milne, she handed several cups of good strong tea, then proudly led them round the rooms and told them that she would like to go on living there as their employee. By the time she packed them off home she had enchanted these connoisseurs and *cognoscenti* of the Trust. It was as if they had fallen under the spell of their school matron. Mrs Laden was quite authoritarian in her way, yet she knew her place and unlike Loewenstein would be in every way a credit to them. In every way except one. For as Loewenstein reminded them, the Trust would have to pay her a salary whereas he would be paying a yearly rent. Here was the plot of a Trollope novel. 'This is going to be a very difficult problem,' concluded Jack Rathbone.

G.B.S. had often emphasized the power of money in his cautionary tales of capitalism, his treatises and treasure hunts for the stage. The story of his posthumous affairs was also largely directed by money motives. Money was granite and rainbow, the practical means to an end and a fabulous end in itself. By the beginning of 1951 the National Trust thought it saw a way of reconciling ends and means by paying the £1,500 costs of the Shaw Memorial Fund Appeal (equivalent to £20,000 in 1990) in exchange for being given first call on the fund when the donations came in. 'I am sure a national appeal, possibly even an international one, is the answer to the difficult financial problem,' wrote Jack Rathbone.

Having invested its hopes in this appeal the Trust was free to appoint Mrs Laden as first custodian of Shaw's Corner. Though 'much appreciative' of Loewenstein's vicarious offer of £500 a year, they 'could not see their way to accepting it,' Jack Rathbone wrote, 'at any rate for the time being'.

All the protagonists were at the house for the opening garden party in March 1951 – Stephen and Clare Winsten, Blanche Patch, Mrs Laden, the officers and gentlemen of the National Trust, and Dr Loewenstein with a squadron from the Shaw Society. So Shaw's Corner took its place with the houses of Carlyle, Kipling and Wordsworth, with Coleridge's, Hardy's and Meredith's cottages, in a special category of properties preserved not for their architectural merit but for their association with great writers. Here was Shaw's workshop, wrote the drama critic Ivor Brown, and 'the workshop of a great man has its vivid associations and abiding interest'.

*

'Mrs Laden is doing wonderfully,' a National Trust memorandum noted soon afterwards. Yet she could not get accustomed to the place without Mr Shaw. It was no longer 'Shaw's Corner', she used to say, but 'Everybody's Corner'. At the same time G.B.S.'s presence grew intensifyingly real to her. She kept on expecting to see him sitting at the dining-room table or appearing at the kitchen hatch to ask her for something – indeed she almost felt 'I was seeing his ghost at times'. When she considered how he would have disliked all these strangers messing up the floors with their muddy boots and dropping tickets everywhere, she could not help getting depressed. Before the end of the year she resigned as custodian and went home to Scotland. 'She plans to add to the recent spate of Shaviana with a book on the years she spent with Shaw,' reported the *Birmingham Post*. Twenty-two years later she served up her intelligent man's guide to the kitchen, *The George Bernard Shaw Vegetarian Cook Book*.

In the first twelve months after Shaw's death almost 20,000 people had come to see the house, producing a surplus of nearly £3,000 (equivalent to £40,000 in 1990), and in the following year over 10,000 visitors arrived raising another £1,000 (equivalent to £12,000). After paying all expenses the National Trust would have been solidly in profit had it not spent its resources hunting that crock of gold at the end of the Memorial Appeal. 'A full report on the failure, with no bones made about who was responsible, could make good reading,' suggested the *Manchester Guardian*. Did this failure simply mark the decline of a writer's reputation after death? Was it particularly steep after such a long public career? 'Shaw's greatest publicity agent died with him,' commented the *Evening Standard*. Or did the start of thirteen years of Conservative government in Britain make these times peculiarly hostile to G.B.S.? Some believed that the death of George VI early in

February 1952, so soon after the official launch (already delayed until after the general election of 1951), was fatal to its chances. Others thought that the medley of squabbling and indifferent members of the Shaw Memorial National Committee was chiefly to blame. Then there were those who blamed the house itself. 'I cannot help wondering whether there are not other houses in England, falling or likely to fall into decay, of historic interest and of beauty without and within, which have a greater claim upon our generosity and self-denial,' mused T. S. Eliot.

From letters sent to the National Trust it is clear that the public misunderstood Shaw's reason for providing the Trust with 'not a single penny' to endow the upkeep of his gift. They believed this proved his fundamental meanness. They did not recognize the paradox of a secretly generous man. Shaw wanted his money to go as far as possible, reaching a considerable number of individuals and institutions. He had given valuable possessions to the National Theatre, National Portrait Gallery, London School of Economics, Fitzwilliam Museum, Tate Gallery, the Metropolitan Museum in New York, the National Library and Municipal Gallery in Dublin. He feared that there might not be enough funds left in his estate for all the annuitants among his employees and family, as well as for the Royal Academy of Dramatic Art, the National Gallery of Ireland, the library department of the British Museum – and his pet alfabet.

The National Trust's deficit had risen in 1950 from £31,000 to £56,000 (equivalent in 1990 to about £800,000). This followed the government's failure to implement a recommendation of the Gowers Report that direct relief from taxation should be granted to owners of historic country houses in return for an undertaking to open them to the public. 'We cannot afford to run this property at a loss,' stated a National Trust memorandum on Ayot St Lawrence. To offset possible loss the Trust sold at auction some of Shaw's silver for £547 (equivalent to £6,500 in 1990), then some furniture for £145-13s-6d, and then again more furniture (including Shaw's pianola for £1-12s-6d) and photographic equipment. It was also given the £416 raised by the appeal. 'Considerable competition' allegedly existed for Mrs Laden's post. Eventually, the second custodian of Shaw's Corner was appointed: a retired police officer then serving as steward to the Conservative Club in Sevenoaks.

This bizarre choice, bringing to mind Miss Patch's odd proposal less than eighteen months earlier, once more passed over the claims of Loewenstein who was never again considered as a National Trust curator. 'Shaw expresses no wish in his will that Loewenstein should live at Shaw's Corner,' Jack Rathbone had written, 'and we have a free hand, except for finance.'

Financially Shaw's Corner continued to be so famously difficult that the Shaw Society ran an ironic advertisement soliciting offers (in the spirit of Act II of *The Apple Cart*) for its complete removal to New England. Attendance fell to fewer than 7,000 visitors a year. Then, following its temporary closure, the house was leased to a private American tenant, C. J. Casserley, and reopened in 1957 by Blanche Patch. Casserley had offered to take this 'millstone round your neck' on condition he need open it to the public no more than once a week and keep a percentage of the admission fees. In lieu of rent he developed the habit of making sensational discoveries of priceless Shavian items that everyone already knew were there. After a year, the National Trust instituted proceedings against him for rent arrears of £250, and he surrendered the lease, throwing in some garden tools as part payment but leaving without settling the rates. The ex-policeman was quickly reinstated, but after his death Clare Winsten's statue of Saint Joan was stolen from the garden in April 1968 and later found damaged beyond repair. It was a nadir in the fortunes of Ayot.

Since no one seemed eager to live among Shaw's possessions and open the place to visitors, maintain the garden and pay rent, a separate flat was made for private tenants incorporating the housekeeper's second-floor quarters, while the property continued to be administered by custodians who occupied the first floor and used the kitchen on the ground floor. This dual arrangement persisted precariously until the 1970s when an apartment was created on the first and second floors for new tenants. In the 1980s these rooms were redesigned as the custodians' quarters, while some of the first-floor rooms, the kitchen and scullery were made open to the public.

The fortunes of the house revived. Over thirty items belonging to G.B.S. discovered in the basement of the Public Trustee's Office – including steel spectacles, silver whistle, gold fountain pen, green penknife – were moved to Ayot, and a room was opened for exhibitions of his books and plays. By 1990 Shaw's Corner was open seven months a year and attracting 17,000 visitors at an admission price of £2 for those who were not members of the National Trust. The problem was how to keep the numbers down.

*

Among those who signed the visitors' book in the 1980s were Loewenstein's family. Loewenstein's own fortunes had sunk rapidly in the 1950s. It was all very different from what he expected. Shaw had expressed a wish in his will that 'my Bibliographer Fritz Erwin Loewenstein Doctor of Philosophy and Founder of the London Shaw Society (now residing at Torca Cottage in Saint Albans) whose knowledge of my literary affairs and interest in my reputation qualify him exceptionally for such employment shall be consulted and employed by my Executor and Trustee' whenever his assistance 'may be desirable and available'. Loewenstein's skills were continuously available, and he was naturally disappointed that they were never desired. A rumour also arose that the Public Trustee had denied him 'a small sum (about £100) that he claimed Shaw had promised to him,' the source of this probably being an uncashed cheque for £100 (equivalent to £1,400 in 1990) still among Loewenstein's private papers.

In fact Shaw made three agreements with Loewenstein during the last eighteen months of his life. On 28 June 1949 and again on 17 February 1950 he guaranteed to pay him sums of £1,500 with the proviso that no more than £500 should be paid in any one year 'to ensure the maintenance of the said Fritz Erwin Loewenstein during the said years and also enable him to complete the bibliography of my works and writings on which he is engaged'. The first of these payments in the June 1949 agreement was to be made in 1951, while the February 1950 agreement covered the years 1954, 1955 and 1956. Both agreements were to pass on from Shaw himself to his 'successors in title and assigns'.

Then, on 4 September 1950, six days before he was to fall in his garden, Shaw signed a third agreement guaranteeing Loewenstein yet another £500 a year for three unspecified years. This third document is similar to the first two, neither of which is referred to or revoked, giving rise to a suspicion that one of the previous agreements had passed from Shaw's memory. All three agreements were witnessed by Mrs Laden and the few variations that appear in the last one seem to have arisen from the making of Shaw's will which was completed on 12 June 1950. He uses the words 'my Executors Administrators assignees and successors' in place of 'myself my successors in title and assigns', and the document ends:

'I charge my estate with the said payments to ensure the maintenance of the said Fritz Erwin Loewenstein and thus enable him to complete his bibliography of my works and writings upon which he is professionally and independently engaged.'

With a total of £4,500 to be paid between 1949 and 1959 (equivalent to £8,000 a year or over £60,000 altogether in the 1990s), Loewenstein's maintenance seemed reasonably secure, especially if he were living at Shaw's Corner. But he was never to receive this money. That Shaw intended to provide for Loewenstein's needs over at least six and possibly nine years is plain to the ordinary reader of these documents. Yet deep obscurities began to unravel themselves before the eyes of trained experts. For Shaw had drafted these agreements, in all their bewildering clarity, without benefit of lawyers. Although they looked and sounded legal, thoroughly legal, it was within the powers of experienced counsel, men who had eaten their dinners and taken silk, to fish up profound uncertainties as to whether they actually formed binding contracts. Indeed it was impossible, they eventually agreed, to decide the matter one way or the other.

Behind this dilemma was the fact that the Public Trustee did not want to pay Loewenstein. It was obvious that his bibliography was of no pecuniary interest to Shaw's estate. In other ways too he was becoming an irritating financial liability. For example, Shaw had given his bank a guarantee for £3,000 in the late 1940s so as to enable Loewenstein to take the tenancy of Torca Cottage in St Albans. In the summer of 1951 the Public Trustee found himself obliged to pay £2,775-0s-4d (equivalent to almost £40,000 in 1990) in settlement of the bank's claim.

Perhaps it was this disagreeable transaction that stiffened the Public Trustee's determination not to pay out the £500 a year stipend during the 1950s. He contended that since Loewenstein was doing little to fulfil his side of the commitment there was an absence of valid consideration, and consequently no legal contracts existed. Loewenstein, who had a shopping bag bursting with bibliographic cards, challenged this contention. He then started litigation proceedings, though somewhat undermining his case by making it known at a meeting of the Shaw Society on 23 November 1952 that he had 'forsaken his bibliographic commitment'. While lawyers analysed the agreements, he sold his large assemblage of Shaviana and his wife opened 'Ann's Pantry' selling continental cakes and coffee in St Albans. Then with some bitterness he took his family in 1955 back to Germany where, as a refugee from the Hitler regime, he was entitled to approximately £2,000 compensation. Finally, on 17 June 1956, while living in Frankfurt, he accepted in full settlement of his claim on Shaw's estate a Court Order for £600 (equivalent to £6,000 in 1990).

*

For almost half a lifetime Fritz Loewenstein, Doctor of Philosophy, had rejoiced in the title of Shaw's 'official Bibliographer & Remembrancer'. But it was for the creation of the Shaw Society that he was himself chiefly to be remembered. Shaw had given this Society four years of life at most and 'it has been the great pleasure of the members to prove him wrong,' wrote T. F. Evans in the twenty-fifth anniversary of the Society's journal *The Shavian*.

Loewenstein's place in the Shaw Society had been filled by a vivacious actor-librarian called Eric Batson who gradually built up the membership until the thousandth member was enrolled in 1963. Though it was never the 'centre for Shavian Thought' Loewenstein visualized, the Shaw Society became for a period the custodian of Shaw's reputation. Batson seemed to know everybody and was immensely popular. He organized meetings that often ended in uproar, inaugurated full-dress play performances in the garden at Ayot on Shaw's birthday each year and made *The Shavian* a journal of peculiar intelligence. In its pages readers could inquire as to their proper response to *My Fair Lady* which was so delighting the public everywhere and would so have exasperated G.B.S. An ingenious solution was proposed by Eric Bentley who recommended Shavians to go and enjoy the first act but then leave at the interval – so missing the descent into conventional romance – and sell their tickets to the non-Shavians still queuing outside the theatre.

It was Batson who 'taught me how to campaign', remembered Barbara Smoker, 'and how to be effective in all sorts of ways'. He marshalled his most spectacular campaign against the Public Trustee whom he suspected of conniving with the Society of Authors (which acts as literary agent for the Shaw Estate) to restrict performances of *Pygmalion* on stage, film, radio and television for up to ten years so that *My Fair Lady* might have a clear run. In Clause 7 of his will, Shaw had written that the Public Trustee should not 'be bound by commercial considerations exclusively it being my desire that he shall give due weight to artistic and public and human considerations...' It was plain to Batson that the Public Trustee had taken absolutely no notice of Shaw's wishes, and was imposing a new type of commercial dictatorship. So he briefed the Member of Parliament for St Pancras South, Lena Jeger (later Baroness Jeger of St Pancras), who brought the matter up before the Attorney-General. Here was further irritation for Sir Reginald Manningham-Buller. He was always having to make sense of Shaw's contentious will. He rose to his feet in the House of Commons and explained that the Public Trustee 'is required by law to administer trusts to the best advantage of the beneficiaries'. Obviously this must mean the best financial advantage. What else? In any case, since the rules of the Public Trustee's Office 'require him to observe strict secrecy,' Manningham-Buller concluded, no inquiry could be made into his administration.

Such secrecy was all Batson required. On behalf of the Shaw Society he formed a 'Not Bloody Likely' committee to prevent the powers of the new Copyright Act from being used as an instrument for censorship. Recognizing that the Public Trustee was too deeply bunkered for attack, he bombarded the Society of Authors. The Society of Authors had denied imposing a ban on *Pygmalion*, admitting merely to 'some form of traffic control ... if congestion and collisions are to be avoided'. But letters of protest from T. S. Eliot, E. M. Forster, Allen Lane, Stephen Spender and many others were soon stacking the correspondence of *The Times*. Was Shakespeare's *Othello* restricted to allow Verdi's *Otello* a clear run? Then Graham Greene announced his resignation from the Society of Authors and urged others to follow him. 'Otherwise we become accomplices in the affair.' Under this threat the Society of Authors made an unacknowledged retreat by allowing several productions of *Pygmalion* to go ahead. The Shaw Society announced a victory and declared a truce.

These were the golden years of the Shaw Society: a period well-furnished with publications by Shaw's surviving friends, beginning with Hesketh Pearson's *G.B.S. A Postscript* and Blanche Patch's *Thirty Years with G.B.S.* in 1951, reaching its pinnacle five years later, the *annus mirabilis* of his centenary, and declining in the 1960s as his remaining friends died and the centre of Shaw studies, growing more academic, moved to the United States and Canada.

4

I take a Shavian to be one who takes nothing on authority, even when the authority is Bernard Shaw.
Brigid Brophy, 'I Never Eat Dead' (1966)

Death appeared to have put little check on Shaw's own literary output. His career hurried on with newly published fiction and criticism, works on music and politics, Shakespearean commentaries, Irish essays, autobiographies and plays (*Buoyant Billions, Farfetched Fables, & Shakes versus Shav* came out in 1951 as the thirty-seventh volume in his Standard Edition). To the serene flow of what are catalogued as 'books and ephemeral publications' were to be added contributions to periodicals and to other authors' volumes, recordings of his broadcasts, his correspondence with Mrs Patrick Campbell, Granville-Barker, Molly Tompkins, Dame Laurentia McLachlan and others. There were additional manifestations and outpourings not to be found in the orthodox canon of his life and works, including eighteen misattributed love poems he never composed for Ellen Terry (according to a graphologist in the 1980s they were written by a woman), some highly original dramas dictated through the ether to sensitively psychic men and women, the appearance of babies attributed to his miraculous interventions at night, simultaneous glimpses of his revisitings from distant parts of the world, all enriching the Shavian apocrypha. To some people it felt as if he were not dead at all. Far from it. 'Shaw has been to my house more than a dozen times since his death,' Frances Day revealed to the *Sunday Graphic* in 1953. '... The first time I thought it was a mouse.'

The Public Trustee had recognized Gabriel Pascal's film rights to a number of Shaw's plays and the newspapers announced his immediate filming of half a dozen masterpieces such as *Man and Superman* in Spain and *Candida* starring Gracie Fields. In 1951 Pascal made a deal for *Androcles and the Lion* in collaboration with the elusive billionaire Howard Hughes who had taken over RKO Studios in 1948. It was to be his first film in Hollywood. Howard Hughes 'has gambled approximately $2,000,000 [over £10,000,000 in 1990] on Mr Pascal's reputation,' announced the *New York Times*. Pascal wanted Chaplin to play Androcles, but this was the McCarthy era and Chaplin, discredited as a communist sympathizer, was unemployable in the United States. The production was to begin with the silent Marx brother Harpo as Androcles and Rex Harrison cast as the Emperor, but these parts were taken over by a young comedian in the Danny Kaye style called Alan Young (following a failed screen test by Frank Sinatra) and the Shavian theatre actor Maurice Evans. Jean Simmons played Lavinia. 'I didn't know what was happening,' she said later. ' . . . [I] didn't know what I was getting into.' The supporting players included a comically miscast Victor Mature as the Captain, a somewhat drunken Robert Newton as Ferrovius, and a lion called Jackie.

It was unlikely material for a Hollywood epic, this story of a Greek tailor who pulls a thorn from the paw of a wounded beast which later refuses to eat him in the Roman Colosseum. Shaw had created a fabulous pantomime and Pascal's ponderous treatment changed his work into the very type of banal melodrama G.B.S. had been satirizing.

Camera work was completed on 17 November 1951 after ten weeks of shooting. Pascal and Hughes 'have yet to meet', the *New York Times* revealed the following day. In their single telephone conversation Pascal had convinced Hughes that G.B.S. would bring 'class' to his lacklustre studio. But Hughes sensed something missing from *Androcles* and, to Pascal's indignation, inserted several scenes of vestal virgins romping round a steam bath.

Before the première, Pascal went out of his way to praise the superiority of Hollywood's technical equipment and the co-operation of the production crew. 'Everybody was anxious for the success of the picture,' he said. Their anxiety was natural. 'As the film went on,' remembered Pascal's wife, 'I began to perspire and shiver at the same time. I had no doubt that it would be ill-received and was going to be a disastrous flop.'

The New York critics were unamused by *Androcles* when it opened at the Capital Theatre in January 1953 and accused Pascal of having 'thrown Shaw to the lions of R.K.O.' 'This is the prelude to my end,' Pascal remarked at the rather grim celebration party in New York. But he put a brave face on it. 'The hell with Shaw and his plays. I want life.' Eighteen months later he was dead. Pursued by mysteriously contending women, haunted by Shaw's spirit, he struggled to keep up his option payments on the musical rights of *Pygmalion* which would miraculously raise him from posthumous bankruptcy. At the Broadway première of *My Fair Lady* in 1956, his widow Valerie Pascal opened her programme and stared at the acknowledgement. 'Adapted from George Bernard Shaw's *Pygmalion*, produced on the screen by Gabriel Pascal.' These lines in small print 'entwining the two names' read like an epitaph on a tombstone, she thought, 'a small memorial to a strange friendship of two dead men'. Shaw, she believed, would have been mischievously delighted.

But Shaw would not have been delighted. Those who named him 'George' usually traduced him. Years earlier a well-known composer and librettist had proposed making a musical of *Captain Brassbound's Conversion* featuring 'a chorus of scallywags, a chorus of Moorish brigands, a chorus for the relieving party ... a chorus for the United States marines ... a chorus of oriental damsels who appeared mysteriously in the garden of the Scottish missionary, and ... a Moorish maiden, who sang an amorous ditty to Captain Brassbound and left the impression that she shared his hours of dalliance.' Altogether, Shaw concluded, 'the play was not as I conceived it, and I declined the honour [and] told the authors that if the thing was produced I'd have the law on them'. As for *Pygmalion*, it had 'its own verbal music' like *Arms and the Man*. 'I have no intention of allowing the history of the Chocolate Soldier to be repeated,' he had insisted. He had got into difficulties over the unauthorized musical of *Arms and the Man* after Siegfried Trebitsch accepted £40 in 1907 (equivalent to £1,500 in 1990) for the right to adapt his German translation of the play into an operetta-libretto for Oscar Straus. Though Shaw sent Trebitsch the £40 with which to repay the librettists, the damage was done. He would not accept royalties from Straus's popular *Der tapfere Soldat*, but he did not have the heart to issue a veto. After that everyone wanted to make a film of it, but 'I will not license the Chocolate Soldier under any circumstances.' In 1941 Trebitsch received an offer of $30,000 from Metro-Goldwyn-Mayer to translate a film scenario if he could get Shaw's authorization. But 'there is no present help nor much future promise in this,' Shaw warned Trebitsch. ' ... I was pledged to Pascal not to allow such a filming, and anyhow it would not have been a decent transaction.' So Ferenc Molnar, the Hungarian playwright, adapted his comedy *The Guardsman* to fit Straus's score for the film version called *Soldier*.

Shaw believed *The Chocolate Soldier* to have been a sentimental travesty of *Arms and the Man* and when Franz Lehár, creator of *The Merry Widow*, proposed making a musical version of *Pygmalion*, he was adamant that such a travesty should not happen again. To all composers he made the same reply and for the rest of his life rejected all appeals to 'downgrade' *Pygmalion* into a musical. 'I absolutely forbid any such outrage,' he wrote in his ninety-second year. This was one battle he believed he had won.

Like the characters in *Widowers' Houses*, Trebitsch and Pascal were caught in the cash nexus. 'I have not the intention to sell Shaw's letters during my lifetime,' Trebitsch wrote to Archibald Henderson in 1953. He had deposited more than 600 of these letters, postcards and telegrams from Shaw in his Austrian bank. They were, he reckoned, worth $100,000. 'I may be *forced* one day to sell, not to let my wife pennyless,' he conceded. Two years after Tina Trebitsch's death, when Trebitsch himself was in his eighty-eighth year, he finally agreed to let the Berg Collection at the New York Public Library purchase his long-held treasure. The end was sad. He 'went to his bank, retrieved the heavy bundle of correspondence, and suffered a heart attack'.

Pascal had briefly been President of the Shaw Society and Trebitsch, who came to London to treat the Society to a special reading of *Jitta's Atonement*, was a Vice-President. *The Shavian* recorded both their deaths: Pascal's in New York on 6 July 1954, Trebitsch's on 3 June 1956 in Vienna. During the 1960s there were regular listings of these deaths of old associates: Barry Jackson in 1961, Sydney Cockerell and Lawrence Langner in 1962, Nancy Astor, Hesketh Pearson and Sean O'Casey in 1964 and, supported by Shaw's annuity at the Onslow Court Hotel, Blanche Patch in 1966. There was also the Secretary of the Shaw Society, Eric Batson. When very young Batson had been epileptic and because of this he was later refused entry into the United States. As he progressed into his late forties he grew strangely volatile. He would incessantly telephone Barbara Smoker and, somehow identifying himself with Shaw, complain about Charlotte's refusal to be a wife to him in the fullest sense while preventing him from having any sexual liaison elsewhere. Another sign of instability was his obsessive hatred of fast cars. At the age of fifty he was confined to a mental hospital for his own protection. But this was in 1965, when wards were being opened up and staff cut down. He had no difficulty in slipping out unseen. Then he threw himself in front of a speeding car and died of multiple injuries.

And so to Loewenstein. While developing his mastery of Mediterranean gardening and an infatuation with the German laws of reparation (which, according to family legend, were improved with his advice) he still maintained connections with the Shaw Society from his homes on the Continent. In 1959 he moved with his wife from Frankfurt to San Remo because it was cheaper and nearer France, and then in 1966 to

Merano in the Dolomites because it was German-speaking and he could live near a synagogue. He remained comparatively poor. During Shaw's lifetime he had written (and G.B.S. rewritten) several articles, published some notes on *An Unsocial Socialist* as well as an eccentric pamphlet on Shaw's rehearsal copies, and seasoned the Shavian legend with *Bernard Shaw through the Camera*. Following Shaw's death, some of his scratchings on the copyrighting of the earlier plays appeared as a supplement to the Shaw Society's *Bulletin*. But after leaving England he published nothing. By the time he died in 1969 a new era of Shavian scholarship was flourishing across the Atlantic.

*

It had begun in November 1952 when, at the Shaw Society, Loewenstein relinquished his bibliography. In the audience that day was a young graduate, a junior colleague of Henry James's biographer and bibliographer Leon Edel, who, having been encouraged by Eric Batson to transfer his interests from Henry James to G.B.S., had recently joined the Shaw Society. Hearing Loewenstein's recantation, he suddenly stood up and affirmed that he would undertake the massive bibliography himself. This young man was Dan H. Laurence who for more than a quarter of a century was to tower over Shaw studies, producing between 1965 and 1988 four scrupulously edited volumes of Shaw's *Collected Letters* and in 1983 a meticulous and comprehensive two-volume Shaw bibliography. These works, together with *The Annual of Bernard Shaw Studies* (an indispensable sign of Shaw's status in the American academies), which is published at Pennsylvania State University State Press under the energetic editorship of Stanley Weintraub, are cornerstones of modern Shaw scholarship.

Shaw had handed over the management of his literary and theatre business to the Society of Authors in 1946. So huge had this business grown, and so complex its scholarly ramifications throughout the world, that in 1973 the Society of Authors issued a press release announcing the formation of an Academic Advisory Committee to help avoid the duplication of projects, and the appointment of Dan H. Laurence as Literary Adviser to vet the use of unpublished material, supervise authentic texts, and guide the publication policy. For half a lifetime Laurence was to work as editorial supervisor on *The Bodley Head Bernard Shaw Collected Plays and their Prefaces* (7 volumes, 1970–74), as general editor of *Bernard Shaw Early Texts: Play Manuscripts in Facsimile* (12 volumes, 1981), and editor of the complete musical criticism, *Shaw's Music* (3 volumes, 1981). He also acted as adviser for some major collectors of Shaw's manuscripts in the United States and in the 1980s as literary adviser to the Shaw Festival at Niagara-on-the-Lake in Canada. From 1970 onwards the quality of editorial work on Shaw prospered with such publications as Stanley Weintraub's two-volume *Shaw: An Autobiography* (1969–70), E. Dean Bevan's ten-volume *A Concordance of the plays and prefaces of Bernard Shaw* (1972), T. F. Evans's *Shaw: The Critical Heritage* (1976), Bernard F. Dukore's *The Collected Screenplays of Bernard Shaw* (1980), the two-volume edition of *The Diaries* annotated by Stanley Weintraub, and A. M. Gibbs's *Shaw: Interviews and Recollections* (1990).

The quantity of academic work also proliferated. By the twenty-fifth anniversary of Shaw's death in 1975 *The Shaw Review* in the United States estimated that in excess of 1,000 articles, more than 100 dissertations and 110 full-length books in six languages had been written on Shaw. There were to be continual additions, among them some amazing curiosities. Items Shaw had excluded from his Standard Edition were added posthumously to this scholarly impedimenta. His ghosted writings for Vandeleur Lee, the 'Practical System of Moral Education for Females' called *My Dear Dorothea* which he composed at the age of twenty-one, his unfinished *Passion Play*, incomplete sixth novel and abandoned work on Soviet Russia, even his Last Will and Testament, were brought to printers and bound into books and pamphlets. All sorts of errant and discarded fragments were rounded up. The evidence on censorship he had given before the Select Committee on the Stage in 1909 was extracted from the minutes and granted separate publication, his marginalia and rehearsal notes reset on centre pages, his uncollected pieces collected, his verses viewed and old reviews re-viewed.

In the 1980s the number of works about Shaw rose to over 300. There were also by this time fifty Study Guides and Notes to his plays issued for students. 'Blast all schools and schoolbooks! They are making literature loathed,' Shaw had written to his publisher in the 1920s when refusing permission to include part of *Saint Joan* in a textbook for the Middle Forms of secondary schools. ' . . . I lay my eternal curse on whomsoever shall now or at any time hereafter make schoolbooks of my works, and make me hated as Shakespear is hated.' This curse was printed as an epigraph to one of the series of revision aids for school examinations.

During Shaw's lifetime the polemical attacks had eventually given way to adulation and anecdotage. The best criticism of his work had been written about his plays-in-performance by contemporary reviewers such as William Archer, Max Beerbohm and Desmond MacCarthy. Already by the late 1930s and increasingly in the period of reaction following Shaw's death, the work of these reviewer-critics had given place to more distant academic assessments. The most influential of these was Raymond Williams's *Drama from Ibsen to Eliot* (1952). Raymond Williams found it difficult to believe that Shaw's 'dynamic as a dramatist can survive its period'. In a revised edition published in 1968 under the title *Drama from Ibsen to Brecht*, he amended 'can' to 'ought to'. The new criticism had little interest in the theatre. Most favourable verdicts on G.B.S. in the 1940s and 1950s had been the work of 'plodding and laborious minds'. In 1947 Eric Bentley described the job of reading books on Shaw as 'a gruelling experience'. Ten years later Kenneth Muir complained that 'there is hardly any serious critical study of his work with the exception of Eric Bentley'.

Eric Bentley brought the fresh intellect of a younger generation to Shaw's work. By the 1960s a new wave of critics, chiefly in the United States and Canada, were turning their attention to the plays and, beginning with Martin Meisel's comprehensive *Shaw and the Nineteenth Century Theater* (1963), producing work of far deeper perception.

Despite the enormous monument raised to him, Shaw's reputation was still insecure and he remained an isolated figure. 'Like Humpty Dumpty he has been fragmented,' wrote the Shavian scholar Margery Morgan, 'and it is almost as hard to put him together again.' One of the few books in which he appeared alongside his contemporaries had been J. I. M. Stewart's *Eight Modern Writers* (1963), the twelfth volume of *The Oxford History of English Literature*. The unusual format covering a period from 1880 to 1940 and containing independent studies of three Irish writers (Yeats and Joyce besides Shaw), an American (Henry James), a Pole (Conrad), a man who escaped England (D. H. Lawrence), the Indian-born Kipling, but no women, drew attention to Shaw's critical awkwardness – the awkwardness of legitimately excluding him or convincingly integrating him into any literary survey.

Shaw belonged equally to the Victorian age and the twentieth century, was part of Irish as well as English culture, and gave forth plays whose prodigality of speech was for a time drowned in the desolate pauses, racked silence, of Beckett and Pinter. Many writers are exiles, as J. I. M.

Stewart implies, but in his posthumous life G.B.S. seemed an exile who had never found another country. He was like a teacher of truants, a collectivist with brilliant individuals for disciples such as Brigid Brophy, Benny Green and Colin Wilson whose work had nothing in common except the leavening influence of Shaw.

In politics too he seemed to be without a constituency, having aligned himself, albeit eccentrically, with the rise of communism that subsequently fell and was by 1991 apparently at an end. What had maddened Shaw was that many of those who supported the Versailles Treaty, who advocated hostility to the Soviet revolution from its earliest days and thereby assisted the rise of nationalist and military dictatorships in the 1920s were later promoted as the champion opponents of Hitler and Stalin. Truly we loved our enemies and felt lost without them. There was in Shaw an immature leaning towards strong men deriving perhaps from the absence of a strong father, and he made frequent stupid and insensitive statements particularly about Stalin in the last twenty years of his life. Like his own surgeon, Cutler Walpole in *The Doctor's Dilemma*, he went on repeating one monotonous and fantastic solution for the blood poisoning of capitalism. Like Shotover in *Heartbreak House* he appeared to batten down the hatches while others were deserting the ship. But his ideal of democratic communism arising from a passionate desire for a more just society based on co-operation rather than competition for profit, was worlds away from the squalid party political regimes of Brezhnev, Andropov and Chernenko that arose after his death. He would inevitably have rejoiced in the dismantling of the Soviet empire and eagerly looked forward to the release and reseeding of all the hopes made sterile in that empire. Whatever happened, he believed that history did not end but was everlasting. He had written optimistically of collapsing systems, inadequate ideologies and the vanishing statues that mark the failing of our dreams in *The Simpleton of the Unexpected Isles*. 'We are not here to fulfil prophecies and fit ourselves into puzzles, but to wrestle with life as it comes. And it never comes as we expect it to come ... Let it come.'

Two remarkable biographies of Shaw appeared within fifteen years of his death. St John Ervine's *Bernard Shaw: His Life, Work and Friends* (1956) had been started a decade before Shaw's death and for almost thirty years this book rather than Archibald Henderson's *George Bernard Shaw: Man of the Century* (1956) was to share with the enlarged edition of Hesketh Pearson's *Bernard Shaw: His Life and Personality* (1961) the function of a standard Life. The other biography was an extraordinary work, *Shaw of Dublin: The Formative Years* (1964) by B. C. Rosset. Rosset was an American in the tradition of Demetrius O'Bolger, that unfortunate 'son of an Irish inspector of police'. He was no writer. His book was a compendium of research and speculation along the network originally threaded by O'Bolger fifty years earlier. But since there was now no disabling help from G.B.S., Rosset was able to do something O'Bolger could not do. He went to Dublin, rented a room in the Synge Street house where Shaw was born, and married the caterer at Trinity College Dublin (who later received an honorary degree for her culinary services). From here he plunged into his investigations round Shaw's home surroundings and came up with some of the discoveries for which O'Bolger had been looking. For example, Shaw wrote that Vandeleur Lee 'had to make his position in London before he could provide the musical setting for my mother and sister'. It was not 'an elopement,' he cautioned O'Bolger, but 'a practical necessity'. Some months, he implied, perhaps a year or two, had separated Lee's departure from his mother's. 'I forget the precise date of the débâcle . . . ' But from the list of departures for Holyhead printed in *The Irish Times* Rosset found the precise dates and the fact that Mrs Shaw had followed Lee to London only a few days after his departure, on her twenty-first wedding anniversary. But the hand of G.B.S. stretched back to shut this book almost as decisively as it had O'Bolger's. Rosset had quoted from Shaw without the permission of the Shaw Estate, and the Society of Authors stepped in to withdraw the book from publication. Not long afterwards, when Rosset died, the repeated history of O'Bolger seemed complete.

*

Seeking equilibrium within contending cultures, the Shaw Estate appeared to have made an alliance between rarefied scholarship and rampant commercialism. In 1963 the profit on *My Fair Lady* was extended when Warner Brothers paid $5,500,000 to the composer-writer team for screen rights. For twenty-four weeks' work while her singing voice was being dubbed, the new Eliza, Audrey Hepburn, was given a salary of $1,000,000. She took the place of Julie Andrews, the star of the stage version (thought by Jack Warner to be unknown by the general public), and, though not nominated herself, was chosen that year (1964) to present Julie Andrews with an Oscar for her performance in *Mary Poppins*.

'Filming *My Fair Lady* was not at all a piece of cake,' Rex Harrison recalled. Under the direction of George Cukor, 'the most famous director of women in the business', an atmosphere of conflict, chagrin and catastrophe quietly filled the studio. But from these rifts and squabbles emerged a well-mannered, slightly pale replica of the theatre musical. This result was partly due to the number of old stagers (Stanley Holloway, Cecil Beaton and Rex Harrison himself) transferred from the Broadway production, and partly attributed to the Shaw Estate which, growing apprehensive after the onslaughts from T. S. Eliot, E. M. Forster, Graham Greene and others, was reported to have 'refused any further excisions in what had once been "Pygmalion"'. Oscars were presented to André Previn for his musical adaptation, to Rex Harrison, George Cukor and Cecil Beaton among others, and fifteen years later, justifying the Shaw Estate's careful policy, the film had earned CBS more than $33,000,000.

The Society of Authors struggled to give respectability to the out-pouring of Shavian productions during the 1950s and 1960s. When Otto Preminger proposed making a film of *Saint Joan* for United Artists in 1956, the Society very happily accepted his choice of scriptwriter, its recent excommunicant Graham Greene. But though both were sincere enemies of Western capitalism, Greene and Shaw seemed incompatible. The seedy population of Greeneland with their painful uncertainties and sinister injustices had no bright quarter for G.B.S. whose cheerful unfamiliarity with the allures of evil eventually made him, to Greene's mind, one of its public agents. Greene had responded to the most anguished of Shaw's plays, *Heartbreak House*, and also loved *Saint Joan* which, 'with a blur of happiness', he associated with his wife Vivien during the months of their engagement. But thirty years later it was no longer sacred to him. So 'I didn't mind adapting his work'.

Preminger wanted someone 'new and fresh' to play Joan, an actress whom audiences could not identify with previous roles. He advertised for a discovery. Eighteen thousand applications arrived and, gathering his bandwagon of publicity, Preminger set off on a crusade round twenty-one cities of the world holding open auditions for this 'Role of the Century'. His search led to a seventeen-year-old chemist's daughter from Marshalltown in Iowa, called Jean Seberg. 'She has the looks, intelligence, feeling and just the right innocence,' Preminger announced. Though she had played a few roles in the local stock company, Jean Seberg was without any professional experience. 'I became very fond of her,' remembered John Gielgud, 'realizing from that first reading what an impossible task must await her.'

Well before shooting started in the new year, Preminger had fixed the date of the première for the second week of May 1957 in Paris and Orléans (with New York and London premières following in June). He preferred to work to schedule, he said, rather than by inspiration. Graham Greene was given six weeks to write his script and, despite crises in the production, including the last-minute withdrawal of Richard Burton as Warwick (replaced by John Gielgud) and of Paul Scofield as Ladvenu (replaced by Kenneth Haigh) as well as the accidental singeing of Jean Seberg at Shepperton studios (witnessed by Barbara Smoker), Preminger faithfully held to his schedule. His *Saint Joan* was a rather glumly assembled 110-minute version of the three and a half hour play, reported *The Times* correspondent in Paris. 'The adapter, Mr Graham Greene, has been at pains to telescope Shaw's argument as faithfully as possible, and the main themes of the trial scene are preserved without fear of offending either theologians or believers in Joan's superhuman freedom from mortal frailty.'

The critics in New York generally treated Greene and Preminger with respect, but were disappointed by the film's lack of spiritual excitement and the failure of its dramatic moments to move them. It seemed a tepid affair, the play's argumentative wit replaced by waves of celestial cinema music. 'I alone am to blame,' declared Preminger. Shaw's *Saint Joan* was 'an intellectual thing,' he regretted, 'it is not a very dramatic play and I found out later . . .'

There were good performances from Gielgud as the coldly impeccable Warwick, Felix Aylmer in the role of the impassive Inquisitor and Harry Andrews as the robustly dogmatic Stogumber. But Preminger was blamed for the miscasting of 'the screen's favourite giggling killer' Richard Widmark playing the sensitive Dauphin, and for the shortcomings of Jean Seberg. The critics described her as 'acting like a ham sandwich' and looking like 'Peter Pan flashing his sword at the pirates'. 'I don't think I ever completely recovered my confidence,' she wrote. Later, through her performance in Godard's *A Bout de Souffle* and her marriage to Romain Gary, she recreated herself as part of the *nouvelle vague* in France. Then she was caught up by the Black Panther Party in the United States. She committed suicide at the end of the 1970s.

The Society of Authors had granted Preminger a licence on condition that changes in the film script did not exceed 24 per cent of the original play. He assured astonished reporters that Graham Greene's version had 'less than 5 per cent deviation, and that is mainly structural not verbal'.

In his Preface to *Saint Joan* Shaw had issued 'Some well-meant Proposals for the Improvement of the Play'. By excising all references to such tedious matters as the Church, he pointed out, to the feudal system, the theory of heresy and so on and so forth, the work could be wonderfully shortened.

'The experienced knights of the blue pencil, having saved an hour and a half by disembowelling the play, would at once proceed to waste two hours in building elaborate scenery, having real water in the river Loire and a real bridge across it, and ... Joan on a real horse. The coronation would eclipse all previous theatrical displays, shewing, first, the procession through the streets of Rheims, and then the service in the cathedral, with special music written for both. Joan would be burnt on stage ... on the principle that it does not matter in the least why a woman is burnt provided she is burnt, and people can pay to see it done.'

This passage, written in 1924, appeared over thirty years later to be an uncannily accurate summary of the Preminger–Greene film. 'The play of course had to be cut for film purposes,' Greene explained in the *New Statesman*, 'but these cuts were mainly drawn from the long discussions on the growth of nationality and the decay of feudalism which would hardly have been understood by film audiences.' But, by taking away the intelligent core of the play, the film blurred its outlines and diminished Joan, the critic Penelope Houston observed, 'into a figure altogether less commanding and fanatical, less formidable and less interesting'.

Graham Greene had been prepared for some salvoes of critical hostility. 'The critics will say another deplorable adaptation,' he wrote, 'though I would defend my script for retaining, however rearranged, Shaw's epilogue and for keeping a sense of responsibility to the author.' He also defended himself strongly against the charge of being brought in to de-Protestantize Shaw's heroine. 'Such a role was never proposed to me nor would I have accepted it,' he wrote. '... There is nothing in Shaw's play offensive to Catholics ... No line was altered for the purpose of watering down Shaw's Protestantism or instilling a Catholic tone.' Evidently Greene did not know of Catholic Action's threat to veto Shaw's own screenplay of *Saint Joan* in the 1930s. What had been objectionable to Catholics then was the depiction of Joan's trial as legally fair and his portrayal of the judges as true representatives of the Church. Greene's additional dialogue appears to get round these difficulties. For he shows Stogumber telling Warwick that particular French priests rather than the Church were responsible for the trial, and he makes Warwick say to Stogumber that Joan will be safely burnt before the Pope hears anything of the matter.

'Anyway I got a few laughs that were not in Bernard Shaw,' Greene later remarked: 'at least I can claim that.'

Some jokes (notably Dubedat's assertion: 'I dont believe in morality. I'm a disciple of Bernard Shaw') were missing from the next Shaw play to be adapted on to film, Metro-Goldwyn-Mayer's *The Doctor's Dilemma* which opened in New York at the end of 1958. Though its screen treatment appeared rather too glossy for some astringent Shavians ('worth seeing for the delphiniums alone,' commented *The Times Educational Supplement*), 'by normal standards of film adaptation, it is remarkably faithful,' *The Shavian* had advised its readers.

With the prospect of bringing Shaw's work before a younger audience, the Society of Authors had made a rather uncommercial contract with MGM, but still reserved rights of approval over the adaptation, choice of director and casting of parts. The screenplay was written by Anatole de Grunwald, 'a very erudite and cultured gentleman', remembered Dirk Bogarde who took the role of Louis Dubedat. '... I never had another script-writer as brilliant until I met Harold Pinter.' Grunwald encouraged the cast to immerse themselves in the original play. But he cut the character of Dr Schutzmacher, the handsome middle-aged Jew who had made his money as a 'sixpenny doctor in a Midlands town', and changed the emphasis of the drama from reflections on the unchanging ethics of Harley Street even after the creation of the Welfare State and its National Health Service to a love story about a scoundrel who was adored by women.

For its director Anthony Asquith *The Doctor's Dilemma* was to be something of an experimental art movie. Converting the female lead from a Cornishwoman into a Breton, he chose the beautiful twenty-six-year-old Leslie Caron, adored as the *ingénue* in *Gigi*, to play opposite Dirk Bogarde (who had recently starred romantically as Sydney Carton in *A Tale of Two Cities*) and, as a further development in the 'Beatonization' of Shaw, persuaded Cecil Beaton to work free of charge designing aesthetic loose-flowing garments for her. These dresses suggested a Pre-Raphaelite atmosphere while concealing Leslie Caron's pregnancy (her daughter was to be called Jennifer after the good-looking Jennifer Dubedat). 'She had to have three sets of each costume because she blew-up and blew-down almost daily.'

Asquith wanted to frame this glamorous young couple with a collection of the very best classical actors then in Britain. 'Shaw's doctors survive the Health Service,' ran an enthusiastic headline in the *Evening Standard*. Critics relished the accomplished performances of Robert Morley fruitily booming away as Sir Ralph Bloomfield Bonington, Alastair Sim, wicked of eye and rolling of tongue as Cutler Walpole, and Felix Aylmer presiding over them with Olympian detachment as Sir Patrick Cullen. The film received good notices. But it was less popular with a cinema public looking forward to seeing Dirk Bogarde in yet another slapstick sequel to Richard Gordon's *Doctor in the House*, and unaware that *The Doctor's Dilemma* was to be a turning-point in his career.

Anthony Asquith, who had directed at least eight films in collaboration with Terence Rattigan and many others deriving from plays (including most famously *The Importance of Being Earnest*), was a director committed to filmed theatre. But he had few visual gifts, little enthusiasm for the drama of ideas, and did not share Shaw's political passions. The question raised by his refined and attenuated version of *The Doctor's Dilemma* was to what extent stage plays were translatable to the screen and whether film makers were at their best directing other people's dramas. 'The subsequent story of Shaw on the screen is generally not a happy one,' noted the critic Donald P. Costello. 'When Shaw films flop, they do it big.' Of the five other films made from Shaw's plays between 1958 and 1968, two never had the chance to 'flop big'. *Helden* was a German version of *Arms and the Man* directed by Franz Peter Wirth in 1958; and *Frau Warrens Gewerbe*, starring Lilli Palmer, was a German adaptation of an original screenplay by Anatole de Grunwald based on *Mrs Warren's Profession* and directed by Akos von Rathony the following year. Neither was shown in Britain or the United States where storms were soon breaking out among accredited Shavians as to which of the last three English-speaking Shaw films really was the worst horror of all.

'*The Devil's Disciple* could have been much better,' admitted Kirk Douglas who played devilish Dick Dudgeon in the Hecht–Hill–Lancaster film of Shaw's melodrama. But the question that troubled many who saw it was: *could it have been worse?* The film was a long-cherished project of Burt Lancaster. He had been trying to make it for over ten years. First he was held up by the arbitrary business habits of Gabriel Pascal, then delayed by the caution of the Society of Authors. But he had put some $800,000 of his own money into it, believing Shaw's play for puritans to be so saturated with off-stage romantic action that it cried out for film treatment. Concentrating on these opportunities for action, the script grew so at odds with the Society of Authors' regulations over limited changes to Shaw's dialogue that its revelation of extreme circumstances bringing out a man's unexpected character vanished.

Immense trouble was taken over this accomplishment. A brilliant British director, Alexander Mackendrick, who had recently made a key film of the 1950s, *Sweet Smell of Success*, revealing the tawdry glamour of the Times Square newspaper world, was hired to replace Anthony Asquith – and then sacked after two weeks because of 'differences of opinion with the producers on how the story should be screened'. Mackendrick, a lifelong admirer of Shaw, had got the point of *The Devil's Disciple* whereas Kirk Douglas and Burt Lancaster, who feared he would 'lose money by making it too highbrow', saw it as a swashbuckling follow-up to *Gunfight at the OK Corral*. Mackendrick's career 'never fully recovered from this dismissal'. He was replaced by Guy Hamilton who amiably gave way to Burt Lancaster. The co-producer Harold Hecht, fresh from having meticulously re-created the English seaside in Hollywood for his film of Terence Rattigan's *Separate Tables*, now went to infinite pains simulating eighteenth-century New England west of London. Colonial buildings designed in Hollywood and then prefabricated in Elstree Studios were hauled along winding Wiltshire roads by 60-foot conveyors and assembled on some acres of muddy gravel-strewn grass at Dyrham Park which was then occupied by a Los Angeles businessman. Here an assortment of actor-dragoons were assisted daily in the authentic complexities of drill and musketry by a young lecturer from Hull University who had been technical adviser on Kirk Douglas's *The Vikings*, while back at Elstree a dialogue director schooled the English cast in correct American parlance.

There was much to make *The Devil's Disciple* a serious candidate for Shaw's worst film. It suffered, wrote a critic in the *Guardian*, from 'the sort of vestigial respectfulness which damages a play without creating an honest-to-goodness film'. The nineteen-year-old Janette Scott, who had been appearing in films since the age of two, was obviously uncomfortable as the ladylike Judith Anderson, while the first sight of Burt Lancaster as her parson husband (generally agreed at the time to be an extreme example of his talent for taking on unsuitable roles) was irrecoverably comic. But the film was partly saved by a *tour de force* from Laurence Olivier as General Burgoyne. He had enormously irritated Burt Lancaster by repeatedly calling him Kirk. But 'in my opinion this Burgoyne is going to run away with the picture,' Burt Lancaster predicted after Olivier completed his part. Kirk Douglas agreed after seeing the première in New York on 20 August 1959. 'Larry Olivier was so brilliant, he stole the picture completely.'

'The cinematic vogue for Shaw continues,' reported *The Times* the following year announcing Shaw's next film. This was the inspiration of an untried producer called Pierre Rouve who wanted Anthony Asquith to direct *The Millionairess* for Twentieth Century-Fox. The Society of Authors agreed on condition that a reliable scriptwriter was chosen to adapt the play. This turned out to be Wolf Mankowitz, a specialist in musicals, who had adapted his own stories 'Make Me an Offer' and 'A Kid for Two Farthings' into films, and whose *Expresso Bongo* had recently featured the nineteen-year-old Cliff Richard as an exploited pop-singer. Mankowitz seemed to offer Shaw's work another opportunity of reaching a young audience. He saw his job as one of making the film into a vehicle for its two stars, Peter Sellers and Sophia Loren.

Peter Sellers was best known for his role as the militant shop steward Fred Kite in *I'm All Right Jack*, and as one of the Goons on radio. Until now he had regarded himself only as 'an ugly-looking comic'. The prospect of playing opposite a sex-goddess who looked 'a lot different from Harry Secombe' dizzied him. Most of the drama took place beyond range of the cameras. Sophia Loren's 'black emeralds' worth £750,000 were stolen; and Peter Sellers, who fainted at the news, went on to break up his marriage under the delusion that Sophia Loren had fallen in love with him – 'I always try to establish a friendly relation with my leading men,' she explained. Realizing that his Indianization of Shaw's serious looking Egyptian doctor could be the opportunity for making an international reputation (the film was actually banned in Egypt but did well in the States), Sellers persistently tried to change the scenes and Anthony Asquith, now at the crumbling end of his career, could not stand up to him. Asquith's technical skill 'has never been in doubt', wrote one critic after the première in London on 20 October 1960. 'The flatness, the slapdash craftsmanship, above all the sheer vulgarity of *The Millionairess* is consequently all the more baffling.' Prolonged superimpositions, frantic cross-cutting and a battery of technical tricks were used to change Shaw's story into an adolescent romp, full of juvenile pranks and haphazard effects but without dramatic cohesion. In the play it is the athletic Alastair Fitzfassenden who 'strips well'; in the film it is Sophia Loren as the Amazonian heroine Epifania who extravagantly undresses. 'This lark,' wrote C. A. Lejeune in the *Observer*, '... can in no way be considered GBS's work.' A few non-Shavian critics rejoiced. You cannot displease everyone all the time. 'As I watched I nearly imitated Mr Khrushchev and began thumping my seat,' wrote Alexander Walker in the *Evening Standard*. 'But not in anger. In delight. Delight at the best film of a Bernard Shaw play since *Pygmalion* – a play that has been refurbished inside and out by Anthony Asquith and now fizzes with effrontery and dances a jig with absurdity.' But according to *The Shaw Review*, Shavians who had been 'so ill-advised or morbidly curious' as to see it could only feel relief that 'the credit line which says "Based on a play by George Bernard Shaw" slips by so fast that if you aren't watching closely you won't see it. It might better say "Based on a title by George Bernard Shaw".'

For most Shavians this was the worst travesty of all. Or so it seemed. But the Irish playwright Hugh Leonard, who scripted *Great Catherine* for Peter O'Toole in 1968, profoundly disagrees. Originally he was commissioned to write two fifty-five-minute screenplays, *Great Catherine* and *The Shewing-up of Blanco Posnet* which were to be shown back-to-back and entitled *The Shavians*. But *Blanco Posnet* soon vanished and Peter O'Toole asked instead for a hundred-minute version of Shaw's Byronic skit with the Battle of Bunker Hill refought on a gigantic set, and much wild Cossack dancing, frenzied chases and general slapstick added for the team of Zero Mostel, Akim Tamiroff, Jack Hawkins, Kenneth Griffith, Jeanne Moreau, Marie Lohr and himself. Gordon Flemyng, whose chief credit was for *Doctor Who* on television, directed the film and the chaos was wonderful. 'Interviewing Jeanne Moreau during the shooting of *Great Catherine*,' wrote a critic from *Sight and Sound*, 'I might just as well have been in the middle of the elephant house at the zoo.' Many of Shaw's bravura jokes still worked well, but Hugh Leonard is adamant: '*Great Catherine* was probably the worst film ever made.'

In all these adaptations, as well as in Pascal's *Pygmalion, Major Barbara* and *Caesar and Cleopatra* made during Shaw's lifetime, there are 'actors looking for sizeable roles, directors seizing upon carefully crafted texts, and producers trying to combine the search for prestige and box office success,' writes the film critic Philip French. '... What none of these pictures has is a director in control of the project who combines visual flair and a genuine interest in ideas.'

'One would like to have seen an Orson Welles film of *Heartbreak House*, with himself as Captain Shotover; Peter O'Toole as Tanner in a film of *Man and Superman* rather than in *Great Catherine*; Stanley Kubrick make a film of *Caesar and Cleopatra* or indeed one of half-a-dozen other plays. The younger contemporary director who could be the right adaptor of Shaw is Peter Greenaway.'

None of Shaw's films, nor the musicals made from his plays, repeated the box office success of *My Fair Lady*, though that success lured many librettists and song writers into prolonged negotiations over *The Devil's Disciple, Major Barbara, Man and Superman*. An American musical of *Caesar and Cleopatra* called *Her First Roman* opened and closed at Boston in the late 1960s, and in the early 1970s Richard Rodgers's charming small-scale adaptation of *Androcles and the Lion*, starring Noël Coward and Norman Wisdom, did not reach Broadway though Norman Wisdom records that 'it was undoubtedly the most exhilarating and excitingly happy experience of my career'. In Britain in the early 1980s a musical version of *The Admirable Bashville* failed to escape from Regent's Park, but dreams were rekindled at Chichester in 1991 and summer aspirations rose on the carnival airs of *Valentine's Day*, Benny Green and Denis King's new musical of *You Never Can Tell*...

*

Though G.B.S. posthumously appeared in several one-man productions and many stage impersonations in concert with Wittgenstein, Wilde, Wells, Yeats, Joyce, Ibsen, Shakespeare and Augustus John, with Isadora Duncan, Marie Stopes and Madame Blavatsky; though he could be seen dancing in a Sadler's Wells ballet, heard singing in a musical by Stephen Sondheim and a musical biography by Johnny Dankworth and Benny Green; though there have been performances of his non-dramatic works such as a theatre version of *The Black Girl* by Christopher Isherwood and the filming of his novel *Love Among the Artists* for television, as well as the dramatic parcelling up of his letters to Janet Achurch, Stella Campbell, Ellen Terry, Kathleen Scott, Margaret Wheeler, Gilbert Murray, Dame Laurentia McLachlan and Sydney

Cockerell, the staple of the Shaw Estate remains the publication and production of his plays.

Every year, for over thirty posthumous years, the number of Shaw plays produced was remarkably consistent. On average the Society of Authors issued twenty-five licences for stock performances in the United States and fifty repertory licences in the United Kingdom. Each year too the number of amateur performances in the United States, as well as those in the United Kingdom, worked out at approximately 1,000. On the European continent and in South America, Shaw's reputation was long tied down by the complex arrangements he had made with his translators (including Trebitsch in Germany, Castelli in Italy, and the Hamons in France). Not until the late 1960s did his work struggle free from these dated versions. Germany, with new translations by Heinrich and Marie Böll, Wolfgang Hildesheimer and Martin Walser all published by Suhrkamp Verlag, produced the largest number of Shaw plays on radio, television and the stage. France, where his plays were brought out by L'Arch Editeur, and Italy, where they were reissued by Arnoldo Mondadori, followed Germany. There was also a marked increase in new Spanish translations and at the beginning of the 1990s a complete edition of his work in Japan.

In Britain, Shaw's plays came and went like sunspots in periodic bursts. Fifteen of them had been put on in London as a public valediction in 1951, and for the centenary of his birth five years later there was a further ten presentations round the country. Between 1964 and 1974 the Society of Authors licensed twenty major productions (excluding repertory performances) of full-length plays and seven of one-act plays. Then in 1975 came another burst of activity with John Schlesinger's staging of *Heartbreak House* at the Old Vic, Simon Callow in *The Doctor's Dilemma* and Stephen Murray in *On the Rocks* at the Mermaid, and Clifford Williams's *Too True to be Good* starring Judi Dench and Ian McKellen at the Globe. The early 1980s, with productions of *Major Barbara* and the full-length *Man and Superman* at the National Theatre, as well as London presentations of *Captain Brassbound's Conversion* with Penelope Keith, *Arms and the Man* with Richard Briers, and *Village Wooing* with Judi Dench, marked another surge of Shavian activity in the London theatre.

There was need for an interlude. Shavian productions had fitted mainly into one of three categories. Often they were used as vehicles for star performers. This practice started in 1951 when Laurence Olivier and Vivien Leigh played *Caesar and Cleopatra* on alternate nights with *Antony and Cleopatra* in London and New York, and it was to end in the early 1980s with Peter O'Toole's 'theatre of comedy' series *Man and Superman*, *Pygmalion* and *The Apple Cart*. 'Many, no doubt, were drawn to this revival of an early Shaw play by the name of Mr Tyrone Power,' commented *The Times* critic reviewing *The Devil's Disciple* in 1956. '... it was the play itself that appeared to take everybody by surprise.' Though there were glorious exceptions including Ralph Richardson's hilarious waiter in *You Never Can Tell* (1966) and Eileen Atkins's formidable St Joan (1977), too many of these star performances – Kay Hammond in *Man and Superman* (1951), Charles Laughton's *Major Barbara* (1956), John Gielgud's infantile Caesar in *Caesar and Cleopatra* (1971), Ingrid Bergman's uncadenced Lady Cicely Waynflete in *Captain Brassbound's Conversion* (1971–2) – were plainly miscast and threw a shadow over Shaw's reputation in the theatre. 'Given his cavalier confrontationalism as dramatist, his fervour as egalitarian moralist,' wrote Susan Todd in the *New Statesman* in 1984, 'it seems unpleasantly ironic that he should have been, for so long now, appropriated by the richest, glossiest, most commercial production companies for what is called "revival." The term suggests the dead, but Shaw's work didn't die. It just got gobbled up, assimilated in the treacly repertoire of plays considered suitable as "star vehicles".'

Yet Shaw's gentility, and the making over of himself as a deliberate wooing of audiences after his 'unpleasant' plays, was partly to blame for such middle-class glossiness. This glossy patina spread over more run-of-the-mill productions. The London theatres filled with a second category of work, the pastime of venerable actors and directors presenting Shaw as a matinée author whose plays could never have shocked and stimulated audiences at the Royal Court Theatre as John Osborne shocked and stimulated them there fifty years later. Few people noticed the family resemblance between Jimmy Porter and John Tanner.

Apart from two or three plays, Shaw's work had never conquered London's West End during his lifetime, nor had it conquered Broadway. The transfer of his early drama from the Royal Court to the Savoy Theatre petered out, and between the wars his place was established in Birmingham and Malvern rather than in London. He grew popular too with touring companies such as the Macdona Players led by Esmé Percy and with provincial repertory theatres at Edinburgh and Glasgow, Chichester and Oxford (where Frank Hauser staged a series of Shaw dramas at the Playhouse). In London he found various homes beyond the West End: in the little 'Q' Theatre built by Jack and Beatrice Leon at the foot of Kew Bridge and the small Everyman Theatre on the hill in Hampstead, at the Lyric Theatre in Hammersmith, Alec Clunes's miniature Arts Theatre in Great Newport Street, and Bernard Miles's Mermaid Theatre at Puddle Dock.

Outstanding productions of his plays nevertheless occasionally appeared in the West End: among them, after many years given over to *My Fair Lady*, a wonderful rediscovery in 1974 of *Pygmalion* at the Albery Theatre directed by John Dexter, with Diana Rigg and Alec McCowen as a dramatically poised, psychologically observed Eliza and Higgins; and two years later, as the Royal Shakespeare Company's celebration of the American bicentennial at the Aldwych Theatre, Jack Gold's tongue-in-cheek exploitation of *The Devil's Disciple* featuring John Wood as the debonair Burgoyne and Tom Conti riding the part of Richard Dudgeon 'like it's a bronco in a rodeo'.

But what original thought went into directing Shaw's work was unsustained. It had promised better. 'The Shaw revival in Britain began on 15 March 1965 with Ronald Eyre's production of *Widowers' Houses*,' Irving Wardle wrote. '... the work itself was quite enough to demolish a whole swathe of Shavian preconceptions and reveal an alarmingly human face under the grinning mask.' But when Ronald Eyre came to direct Shaw's companion piece, *Mrs Warren's Profession*, at the Old Vic at the end of 1970, Irving Wardle conceded: 'lightning does not strike twice in the same place, least of all theatrical lightning; and there are no grand illuminations to be found in this revival'. Again, reviewing Frank Dunlop's vivid production of *Too True to be Good* a few months after *Widowers' Houses*, Irving Wardle predicted in *The Times* that it would be seen as 'a well-calculated act of revaluation designed to open up his neglected last phase'. But despite some promisingly surreal versions of *Heartbreak House* and a heroic experiment with *Back to Methuselah* (1984) conducted by nine actors under the direction of Bill Pryde, Shaw's last phase was never convincingly opened up. Nor, despite a few brilliant individual performances – Ian McKellen in *O'Flaherty, V.C.* (1966) at the Mermaid or in *Too True to be Good* (1975) for the Royal Shakespeare Company – did the London theatre move far into this third category of production and away from the standard Shavian comedies and chronicles. By 1973, after the death of Peter Bridge, a young commercial manager with a flair for bringing Shaw productions to the West End, Irving Wardle concluded that 'the Shavian revival is on the ebb'.

This reflected in part the prevailing post-Brechtian theatre at the Royal Court and a shift in the training methods of actors following Joan Littlewood's revolution at Stratford East. The abandonment, outside Shakespeare, of stylized speech training (with actors practising like singers) in favour of improvisation and realism, and the rise of the actor-director which seemed to clash with Shaw's theatrical ideology of power to the playwright, lay at the root of a growing embarrassment at the National Theatre over its attitude to Shaw. Meanwhile, desperate economies in the commercial theatre increasingly handicapped the productions of plays demanding full casts and changes of sets, and led the way to sparse two-voice texts, the transfer of television material and the more lavish appeal of West End musicals.

But a bolder revival was already taking place in Canada where Shaw's drama had been made popular by Maurice Colbourne and Barry Jones's tours, the expert presentations by the Canadian Broadcasting Corporation, and performances up and down the leading Little Theatres (as the non-professional centres were known). The plays had survived their reputation for being iconoclastic and even revolutionary, and the Anglo-Irish G.B.S. became a favourite entertainer with Anglo-Canadian audiences untroubled by his political convictions.

In 1962 a modest Shaw Festival started in Ontario. Its founder was a Toronto lawyer, Brian Doherty, who (rather in the manner of Barry Jackson at Birmingham) had lost money through his passion for the theatre. Retiring to the small nineteenth-century town Niagara-on-the-Lake, he launched his Shaw Festival with four amateur performances of *Don Juan in Hell* played on weekends in the cramped and suffocating Old Court House. By 1963 the Festival began staging full-length productions. After three semi-professional seasons sustained by the actors' enthusiasm and the commitment of the artistic director Andrew Allan, the venture was 'transformed for ever' in 1966 by the arrival of Barry Morse. He brought showmanship to the Festival. 'Working with Barry,' remembered Brian Doherty, 'was like going over Niagara Falls in a barrel.' There seemed nothing he could not do by way of blandishment, cajolery, the exploitation of friends and the inflammation of strangers. Television audiences saw him seated on a kitchen chair at a card table in the middle of a traffic island prompting questions on his lack of office facilities. As with Malvern during the 1930s, not everyone in Niagara was friendly. 'We encountered bloody-mindedness as well as saintly kindness,' he records, ' – but gradually the town warmed up.' He extended the season to nine weeks and staged three full-length Shaw plays, persuading the local military to fire 'a monstrous rocket from the roof of the building' at their opening performance. The result was a sell-out. 'We sold all the seats we had to sell' – 350 for each show totalling 25,000 seats throughout the season in a town with a population of little more than 5,000 inhabitants (the population of the whole district, including a large part of the north-east corner of the Peninsula, is only 12,000).

The Festival expanded again under the artistic director Paxton Whitehead. A beautiful new rose-coloured theatre designed by the Canadian architect Ron Thom holding 832 seats was opened in the summer of 1973. Seven years later, when Christopher Newton came from the Vancouver Playhouse to take over the directorship, a third theatre, the Royal George, was purchased. Originally built as a vaude-ville theatre in 1913, it had been used to entertain the troops in the First World War and subsequently functioned as a road house, a cinema, and a home for the Canadian Mime Theatre. Restoring the Edwardian décor, the Shaw Festival was to put on its most popular plays, the rediscovered musicals and lunchtime productions there.

Being close to the United States, the Festival could attract audiences from across the border with farces and musical comedies, dramas of romance and detection. It gained a reputation for lightness of heart at the expense of Shaw's darker humour, and during the 1980s made a name for itself with a number of extraordinary productions: *Cyrano de Bergerac*, *Camille*, Brecht's *A Respectable Wedding*, and a controversial *Saint Joan* without the Epilogue. There were unusual Shaw plays too: *The Simpleton of the Unexpected Isles* (1983), *On the Rocks* (1986), *Getting Married* (1989); a haunting *Heartbreak House* in 1985, a memorable *Man and Superman* played with *Don Juan in Hell* in 1989, a triumphant *Millionairess* starring Nicola Cavendish in 1991. 'The standard there is very high indeed,' reported the editor of *The Shavian*, T. F. Evans. *You Never Can Tell* (1988) and *Misalliance* (1990) were, he judged, 'the best all-round productions of the ten or dozen each of these plays that I have seen'. Already by 1980 the Festival had created an ensemble on Euro-pean lines. Lasting eight months of the year, it now imports international directors and presents, besides Shavian drama each year, plays from Russia, France, Scandinavia, Germany, Hungary, Canada and the United States. 'In the last seven years we have scrupulously kept to our mandate of plays written during Shaw's lifetime – nothing else,'

Christopher Newton wrote in 1991. 'It gives us a unique perspective on dramatic literature ... It forces us to look at the old from a new vantage point.' What had begun at Malvern in the 1930s was accomplished in Niagara fifty years later. By the early 1990s some forty-five plays by Shaw had been presented in almost ninety productions, together with work by over a hundred and twenty other dramatists, many of which toured Canada and the United States. A fringe of seminars, special events, and projects for young people sprang up. From the days when actors banged nails into the walls to hang their clothes and dressed in the Court House kitchen or a derelict barn by the parking lot, the Shaw Festival had flowered into a centre for the performing arts and 'one of the most exciting theatrical events on the North American continent,' wrote the *Guardian* critic Michael Billington.

'In Canada, we were less liable to be spotted for cuts of the original,' explained the doyen of Canada's theatre critics, Herbert Whittaker. In Britain, and to some extent in the United States, directors were sometimes intimidated by Shaw's authoritative stage directions and the policing of texts by the Society of Authors' Academic Advisory Committee. It was not always remembered that these stage directions had been added, like the prefaces, as a narrative enabling these works to appear in published form and be read by the public almost as if they were novels. There were also many stories of Shaw's terrific refusals to cut his own plays during his lifetime, which antagonized some directors by seeming to fix a precedent.

But G.B.S. was an apostle of change, adept at bringing his facts up to date. 'If I were you I should cut the part,' he had advised Ellen Terry while she was preparing the role of Imogen for Henry Irving's production of *Cymbeline*. Shaw used Shakespeare like everyone else uses Shakespeare: as an autobiographical code. Towards the end of his life he was telling Dame Laurentia McLachlan: 'I need pruning. There's a lot of dead wood.' He knew that he overwrote and that naturally 'I shall have my period of staleness and out-of-dateness for years after my death.' This reaction was to be compounded by the advent of television with its habit of 'small acting' in front of cameras in place of the flamboyant performances demanded by the Shavian theatre.

'Do not treat my printed text with blindly superstitious reverence,' Shaw told a producer when in his nineties. 'It must always be adapted intelligently to the studio, the screen, the stage, or whatever the physical conditions of performance may be.' During his posthumous period of staleness there was far too little intelligent adaptation, too much super-stitious reverence. The première of *Geneva* with its extra act was given at the Mermaid in 1971, but seven years later the director Christopher Morahan was refused permission to add the original unperformed last act of *The Philanderer* to his imaginative production at the National Theatre in London, and the chance of seeing a substantially new play was further delayed. In the last decade of Shaw's copyright, however, the Shaw Estate has allowed a world première of the full-length *Philanderer* at the Hampstead Theatre (1991) signalling a new opportunity for Shaw on stage.

The difficulty in presenting Shaw's plays to modern audiences is not simply a matter of pruning texts and transcending acting fashions. It is also a matter of deciding what sort of plays he wrote. Borges praised him for creating superb characters on stage, Brecht for subverting character and introducing the spirit of alienation. 'As an imitator of Ibsen, Strindberg, Chekhov or Shakespeare,' wrote Margery Morgan, 'Shaw produced work that impresses us much more by its differences from his models, radical differences of tone and quality, than by the detectable similarities.' These differences have led to a confusing divergence of critical opinion.

Shaw's originality depends on a peculiar vision which has been likened to El Greco's astigmatism. In his Preface to *Plays Unpleasant*, he had written of 'having got a clue to my real condition' from an ophthal-mic physician who 'tested my eyesight one evening, and informed me that it was quite uninteresting to him because it was normal ... normal sight conferring the power of seeing things accurately, and being enjoyed by only about ten per cent of the population, the remaining ninety percent being abnormal.' Shaw uses this story to establish his credentials as a 'realist', but as his method of telling the story shows he was no more realistic or 'natural' in his way of thinking than Hamlet (to whom he sometimes likened himself), though his 'mind's eye' has something of the same ingrained theatricality.

> HAMLET: My father, methinks I see my father.
> HORATIO: O where, my lord?
> HAMLET: In my mind's eye, Horatio.

Shaw's mental vision, which 'saw things differently from other people's eyes, and saw them better,' was an example of what ophthalmic opticians would now call antimetropic sight: one eye focused short, the other long.

This is what Shaw himself was indicating when he told G. K. Chesterton that an Irishman had one eye for reality and the other for poetry. In his earlier plays he had begun by looking at his contemporary world, singling out themes of recurring topicality – feminism, disarmament, medical and marital ethics, property values versus human values, the relationship between Ireland and England, the peaceful invasion of Britain by the United States, the rise of trade union power. In sociological and political terms, 'almost all of Shaw's plays are at almost all times timely,' Sheridan Morley wrote when reviewing *Misalliance* in 1973. 'He seems to be foreseeing our future,' wrote Alan Brien commenting on *Too True to be Good* in 1975. Being a philosophical dramatist and an acute social analyst, Shaw identified basic unchanging motives and processes. In his later plays he went on to cultivate the long-range outlook that strengthened his impersonal habit of mind, training his eye for poetry into a prophetic gaze that seemed to stare 'through you or over you', Leonard Woolf noticed, 'into a distant world or universe'. This abstract view became part of his special equipment in the theatre, enabling him to use ancient theatrical forms to present contemporary themes.

Only the most flexible direction, which recognizes that Shaw sometimes worked in several genres within the same play, can bring together the various movements of his work. Drama was for him a broad spectrum that terminated at one end in opera (he considered Shakespeare's *Othello* as essentially a musical melodrama). 'My method, my system, my tradition, is founded on music,' he wrote. Seeking a rhetorical notation based on music pitch and dynamics, bringing musical ideas to acting, using operatic allusion to play up romantic sentiment and operatic conceptions to shape his scenes as overtures, arias, duets, ensembles, Shaw's theatre of ideas calls for the opera-inspired direction given by Richard Jones to the work of Corneille and Ostrovsky, and by Steven Pimlott to Molière's *The Miser* in the early 1990s.

*

'The man's life and works are either nothing or they belong to the future,' wrote Eric Bentley in 1951. Shaw's life and works were rightly challenged after his death by later generations demanding a close examination of both before accepting him as one of their representatives in history.

In 1970 the Shaw Estate decided to commission an authorized biography to complement the critical exploration of his dramaturgical techniques and the relationship between his art and politics. 'All the biographies so far have been partial,' explained Elizabeth Barber, General Secretary of the Society of Authors, in an interview for *The Times*. 'St John Ervine in 1956 was the most comprehensive, but the time has come, the estate feels, for an assessment of the man in his period.' There was some wonder, however, mixed with consternation, when scholars found that the wheel had stopped with its arrow pointing at a biographer who had no experience of politics or theatre, no academic qualifications, and no record of having worked on Shaw.

I was thirty-four and this experience was certainly new for me. I was then writing the Life of a flamboyant heterosexual, having previously published books about a notorious homosexual and an unknown impoverished writer who, following the appearance of my book, stubbornly remained unknown. People usually implored me not to write biographies of their friends and members of their family. Now I was gaining respectability, albeit controversial respectability. The feeling was not altogether comfortable. This invitation from the British Museum, the Royal Academy of Dramatic Art, and the National Gallery of Ireland was obviously a great honour, but it was also a considerable terror. To my eyes G.B.S. appeared a gigantic and incomprehensible figure with whom I felt little intimacy, yet this was a challenge I really ought to accept. Nevertheless I hesitated. I had heard that Shaw wrote ten letters a day, every day, all his adult life, and that people kept his letters. I knew that he had composed more than fifty plays, that there was a collected edition of almost forty volumes, and many library yards of books about him, as well as huge deposits of unpublished papers around the world. I began to suspect that with his shorthand and his secretaries G.B.S. could actually write in a day more words than I could read in a day. Since he lived into his mid-nineties working vigorously to the end, this was an alarming prospect. I therefore prevaricated. Having recently begun research for a life of Augustus John I was able to advance this as a proper reason for being unable to start on G.B.S. until the mid-1970s. The Shaw Estate was unmoved.

In 1975 I began my Shavian research in Dublin. Here I found there was almost no one who, even when they had no information at all, would not be prepared to volunteer something over a jar or two. For a long time I was encumbered with help. People I had never heard of came to my door to advise me sympathetically that they knew nothing. Many wrote letters to the same effect: some hopefully in verse; others more prosaically enclosing business cards. One lady wanted to know whether Shaw's biographer could obtain an introduction for her to the Royal Family. Everyone pressed in on me so warmly that I was moved to reply with such politeness that my replies elicited answers to which I felt bound to respond. One lady (whom I never met), noting the volume of our correspondence over the years, ventured to ask whether we had ever had an affair, the crucial part of which had escaped her. I was swimming in the wake of the great Shavian legend. Eventually I found myself pursuing G.B.S. to Soviet Russia, New Zealand, Italy, South Africa, and also to many places he had never been but which now held his manuscripts. There is a Shaw Collection at the British Library: there is a Shaw distribution throughout the world.

It took me some three years to get a sense of breaking Shaw's literary code, the alpha and omega of his dramatic style, and picking up subtle underlying themes which, to reach an immediate public, he had orchestrated for trumpet and big drum. Many people had come to think of G.B.S. as having only ink in his veins and having been born with a long white beard. I have tried to dismantle this bearded literary superman and replace him with a more recognizable if still uncommon human being. Behind the public phenomenon was a private individual, infrequently glimpsed, who gives G.B.S. his concealed humanity. He covered up his vulnerability with dazzling panache: I have tried to uncover it and, without losing the sparkle of this panache, show the need he had while alive for such brilliant covering. He has been an unsettling companion, stimulating, exasperating, who uses all his powers of lucidity and dark exhilarating humour, to challenge orthodoxies, subvert conventions, uproot fashion and make us see an alternative view. This is an honourable function of literature. His childhood and adolescence had been rich only in dreams, he told Ellen Terry, frightful and loveless in reality. It was the dreamer who went on to write plays and the man who wanted to make the realities of the world less frightful who played with politics. 'Live in contact with dreams and you will get something of their charm: live in contact with facts and you will get something of their brutality,' he wrote in *John Bull's Other Island*. 'I wish I could find a country to live in where the facts were not brutal and the dreams not unreal.'

There is such a country and its name is Utopia. 'A map of the world that does not include Utopia,' wrote Oscar Wilde in *The Soul of Man Under Socialism*, 'is not worth glancing at.' For some tastes there is not enough evidence of love in Shaw's Utopia. 'I implore you not to describe me as a loveable human being,' he appealed to Lawrence Langner. But he had also written: 'let those who may complain that it was all on paper remember only on paper has humanity yet achieved glory, beauty, truth, knowledge, virtue, and abiding love.' He wanted people to grow more self-sufficient rather than depend for their vital happiness on the off-chance of romance, with its partiality, favouritism, unfairness, and abiding penalties. What existed as sentimentality in others was turned within him into political idealism. He became a saint of the lonely and the fugleman of those who were out of step with their times. He gave them a heartening message. For every disadvantage, in Shavian terms, becomes a potential asset in disguise. The art of life is the art of heroic paradox. But under the play of his paradoxes, between his life and the work, moves a current of passion, often diverted and running with ironic cross-currents. It is this that I have sought to navigate.

Shaw objected to biography in his time because, by presenting 'barren scoundrels as explorers and discoverers', it glamorized the past and idealized a corrupt system. As a young man in the 1880s he had called for the revolution in biographical writing that was to be pioneered by Lytton Strachey. A little later, in 1905, Shaw wrote to Henry Irving's son: 'If you write a life of your father, don't make it a vestryman's epitaph. Let us have the truth about the artist ... The artist sacrifices everything to his art, beginning with himself.' Later, when infiltrating the work of his own biographers with concealed autobiography, he sacrificed something of his life so that these books might act as endorsements to his political commitments and avoid giving pain to living people. But he had also acknowledged that 'no man has an accurate knowledge of his own life & that when an autobiography does not agree with a biography, the biography is probably right and the autobiography wrong'.

Treating the gospels as early examples of biography Shaw noted in the Preface to *Androcles and the Lion* how St Matthew ('like most biographers') tended to 'identify the opinions and prejudices of his hero with his own', while St John used biography as a record of the 'fulfilment of ancient Jewish prophecies'. He concluded: 'When you read a biography remember that the truth is never fit for publication.' Since Shaw's death, biographical technique and subject matter have expanded so that biography now embraces the whole range of human experience, in so far as it is recoverable, and accepts it as fit for publication. I do not specifically identify my opinions and prejudices with Shaw's so far as I am aware, nor have I used his life to record the fulfilment or non-fulfilment of socialist prophecies. My deepest involvement is with biography itself and its never-ending love-affair with human nature, and my aim has been to come a little nearer a biographical ideal described by Hugh Kingsmill as 'the complete sympathy of complete detachment'.

POSTSCRIPT

I must stop, leaving much unsaid ... I have gone on as far as I am able.
Everybody's Political What's What?

The Last Laugh commences with Shaw's death and finishes with the publisher's deadline. This short postscript follows precedents from G.B.S. himself who tied last-minute scenes into *Geneva*, his harlequinade on the rapid developments of contemporary politics; and it will end rather as he ended the Envoy to *Everybody's Political What's What?* – after which he went back and inserted an extra act into *Geneva*.

*

The first Bernard Shaw Summer School was opened in Dublin on 21 June 1991. This three-day event, putting many surprising participants (from Roy Hattersley MP to Seamus Heaney) through their paces, was crammed with seminars, suppers, film shows, music, theatre, and had been the inspiration of Cornelius Howard, a lunchtime legend at the Department of Foreign Affairs where until recently he had managed Irish cultural relations with the rest of the world.

'Money talks: money prints: money broadcasts: money reigns,' wrote Shaw in his Preface to *The Apple Cart*. The Festival Programme contained an urgent appeal for money from the chairperson of the Shaw Birthplace Trust, Nora Lever. She was a woman with two telephones. On one she indulged her Shavian passion; on the other she exercised her compassion for Dublin's stray cats. During the late summer of 1991, the stricken Irish cats were obliged to wait their turn in the streets while the professor set her trustees on to the Taoiseach, Charles Haughey. 'It could only happen in Ireland', she lamented, 'that during the year in which we celebrate our European Cultural Capital status, we have to beg for money to rescue the house of a Nobel Prizewinning writer.'

Nora Lever's begging powers were formidable, but then so was the financial plight of 33 Synge Street. With help from the American Women's Club of Dublin, one room had already been refurbished and opened by President Mary Robinson with an evening of Victorian music.

But elsewhere the ceilings sagged, walls crumbled, and there was an odour of decay. 'In fact it's a wreck,' pronounced Professor Lever when inviting journalists to 'Come in, and see the devastation.'

With an overdraft of more than £50,000 it could only be a matter of weeks before the bank foreclosed and put the property back on the market. But Nora Lever made sure that the unfortunate Taoiseach was continuously beset with questions, petitions, suggestions, appeals. 'We would like to be as generous as we can about these matters,' he pleaded. He was saddened to hear the government's indirect allocation of £10,000 through the Irish Sailors' and Soldiers' Land fund dismissed as 'derisory'. Yet it was certainly true that the amount of money needed to convert the house into a museum and international centre for students would be less than the Shaw royalties that went to the National Gallery of Ireland in one year – royalties that in recent times appeared to have been used for purposes normally financed out of central government funds.

Nora Lever spread the campaign into British and American newspapers, commandeered as trustees some of her fiercest stray-cat colleagues, obliged the bank to grant a short extension, and called a press conference. It would be 'monstrous' declared the *Evening Press*, a 'disgrace' announced the *Sunday Press*, a 'national disgrace' agreed the *Irish Press*, if Ireland failed to honour Dublin's debt to G.B.S.

On 23 October, acknowledging that he had been 'made aware' of the difficulties of the Shaw Birthplace Museum Trust, the Taoiseach promised in the Dáil to allocate 'a further grant of approximately £54,000 also from the Irish Sailors' and Soldiers' Land Trust to complete the purchase of the property'.† So the house was saved and the Taoiseach happily prepared to leave office.

*

On 14 November, almost one hundred years after its composition, the world première of a Shaw play opened at the Hampstead Theatre in London.

In 1893, when Lady Colin Campbell had persuaded him to cancel his original last act of *The Philanderer* because it was then impossibly far ahead of its time, Shaw had written another act that could be performed either as an alternative end, substituting a conventional marriage for a

---

†Following a restoration appeal, launched with a brochure from Penguin Books, the Shaw House was signed over to Dublin Tourism on 15 September 1992. It will be opened as a museum in 1993, with furniture provided by the Shaw Trust. Meanwhile the three-year-old Shaw Society of Dublin prospers and flourishes.

happy separation, or (once public opinion found his unorthodox treatment of divorce acceptable on stage) as a penultimate act which lent extra irony to his original conclusion.

'They think this a happy ending, Julia, these men: our lords and masters!' he makes Grace Tranfield say during the additional act. But when publishing *The Philanderer* as one of his 'three Unpleasant Plays' in 1898, Shaw printed only this implausible 'happy ending' as his finale, moving the comedy nearer the traditional Victorian farce. This, too, was the version that, with a few revisions, reappeared over thirty years later in his Collected Edition. 'I make no attempt to bring the play up to date,' he wrote in a prefatory note of 1930. Nowhere is there any mention of the missing act. Much of what he had intended to pour into the full-length play he had by that time decanted into other plays. He had transformed the philanderer Leonard Charteris into John Tanner, the Don Juan of *Man and Superman*; re-examined Dr Paramour's medical ethics in *The Doctor's Dilemma*; exposed the restrictions of conventional marriage in *Getting Married*; and pursued the new disquisitory trail first attempted in the cancelled act through *Misalliance* and *Heartbreak House*.

The Philanderer had been an unhappy work, stirring up memories of his unfortunate affair with Jenny Patterson, forcing compromise on him to no avail, and fitting awkwardly between *Widowers' Houses* and *Mrs Warren's Profession*. He had apparently put the abandoned act out of his mind and it was unknown to his contemporaries. After his death, it found its way as part of the Shaw Collection into the Department of Manuscripts at the British Museum. It was first published in facsimile in 1981, though it has never been printed and was not seen on stage until the actor Brian Cox decided to direct it at the Hampstead Theatre.

The question was whether the complete version would succeed as intellectual comedy in the theatre and restore *The Philanderer* to its full weight as one of the three 'Plays Unpleasant'. The critics were pretty well unanimous. In *The Sunday Telegraph* John Gross described the new material as a 'welcome addition' and the four-act play as a 'decided success'. 'It gives a much-needed Ibsenite irony and bite,' wrote Michael Billington in the *Guardian*, '... This is good hard-hitting stuff'. In *The Times Literary Supplement* David Trotter argued that, by releasing it from the limitations of topical comedy, 'the fourth Act makes *The Philanderer* a much better play', and Christopher Edwards in *The Spectator* wrote that it now 'ends on a note that is worldly, humane and honest about marriage ... the insights Shaw advances touch upon something universal in sexual relations'.

*

During the last six months of 1991 Shaw produced only one new massive book: a five-hundred-page volume bringing together his contributions between 1885 and 1888 to the *Pall Mall Gazette*, lavishly edited by Brian Tyson and entitled *Shaw's Book Reviews*. But G.B.S. has by no means slacked off. There is a substantial load of fresh works by him being conveyed via scholars to the printers, in particular a dozen additional volumes of his correspondence with William Archer, Nancy Astor, John Farleigh, Augustin Hamon, Gilbert Murray, Gabriel Pascal, H. G. Wells, Lady Gregory, Margaret Wheeler – and Charlotte's correspondence with T. E. Lawrence.

There has also been considerable activity in the manuscripts market. In November a wide-ranging collection of Shaw materials formed by an internationally known Shavian scholar, Sidney P. Albert, was acquired by Brown University in the United States; and in London, on 12 December, the *New Statesman* archive went under the hammer as part of a Sotheby auction in which the Shaw manuscripts, exceeding their estimates, fetched £18,450. The year culminated with the spectacular discovery of the original letters from Shaw to Ellen Terry. This correspondence had been bought by Elbridge Adams shortly after Ellen Terry's death and printed by his company, the Fountain Press, in 1931 edited by 'Christopher St John', the pseudonym of Christabell Marshall. Her volume contained one hundred and ninety-one letters from Ellen Terry to Shaw with one hundred and eighteen of his to her which G.B.S. revised for publication. (Dan H. Laurence made accurate transcripts of ninety-seven of these from photocopies at the Library of Congress in Washington for his *Bernard Shaw: Collected Letters*.)

The original correspondence was now valued by Bernard Quaritch Ltd for a 'willing seller, willing buyer' price of £75,000 and offered for sale to the British Library. The British Library at once applied to the British Museum for this money to be made available from the Shaw Fund which Parliament was told more than thirty years earlier would be used 'primarily for the benefit of the library'. Since the late 1950s the British Museum had been receiving from the Shaw Estate the equivalent of twice this sum each year for its capital investment fund. In ordinary circumstances it would have taken the British Museum up to five years to contribute so large a sum as £75,000 for British Library heritage purchases. But could it refuse to pay Shaw's money for Shaw's letters? The question was to come before the new Director of the British Museum, Dr Robert Anderson, in the new financial year and he had promised 'some key changes'.

The financial year was less than a week old when the British Museum decided to grant the money for this purchase. Since the British Library had long owned Ellen Terry's letters to Shaw, this fascinating correspondence was finally brought together, and a display put on exhibition in the summer of 1992.

The question remained as to whether this grant signalled a new spirit of co-operation between the Library and the Museum over the Shaw Fund or had been made in special circumstances and 'without prejudice'. Plans by Mark Fisher MP for an Adjournment Debate on the matter in the House of Commons were forestalled by the onset of the spring General Election, and instead Lord Annan inaugurated a short debate in the House of Lords on 27 February. He reminded Lord Astor, Conservative spokesman for the arts, of Edward Boyle's assurances and drew attention to the odd manner in which they had been ignored. He was supported by, among others, Baroness Birk, Lord Jenkins of Putney and Lord Eccles who had managed the Shaw Fund in the 1960s and 'greatly increased its capital'. But the eminent archaeologist, Lord Renfrew of Kaimsthorn, speaking as a trustee of the British Museum, merely stonewalled by inviting Lord Astor to confirm that the Shaw bequest had been technically 'unrestricted' and to agree that the British Library Act 1972 made no specific provision for the transfer of trust funds to the library.

The debate spilled over into the correspondence columns of *The Times*. Despite the case in Chancery against Shaw's alphabet trusts, Lord Renfrew wrote (10 April): 'I do not believe Shaw's wishes to have been ignored (and would be unhappy if they were).' He added that he would have been 'outraged to see Parliament misled'. Though more of Shaw's money had gone on refurbishing the Museum's galleries and modernizing its non-vegetarian restaurant than to the British Library, Lord Renfrew could not see that anything unusual had been dug up. But the extended debate gave the public new information, and the general view, as reported in the newspapers, was that if the Museum was not to appear unconscionably greedy and the Library extremely feeble, then some fairer arrangement must be reached. In the summer of 1992 the two institutions met to discuss the situation...

The year 1992 had started with a vintage production of *Misalliance* by the American Repertory Theatre in Cambridge, Massachusetts, its length beneficially cut by over twenty minutes. In London there was a blitz of revivals, including Alec McCowen in a museum-like *Caesar and Cleopatra* at the Greenwich Theatre, Alan Howard and Frances Barber in a spectacularly staged 'complete representation' of *Pygmalion* (conflating the theatre and film texts) at the Olivier (while *My Fair Lady* toured the country with Edward Fox), Trevor Nunn's grand but unstable production of *Heartbreak House* starring Paul Scofield and Vanessa Redgrave; as well as an exhibition chronicling Shaw's life and work at the National Portrait Gallery.

As to the future – which promises new films of *Saint Joan* and *Mrs Warren's Profession* (scripted by Fay Weldon), the coming of *Valentine's Day* to the West End and, in the United States, an international centennial conference marking the first production of *Widowers' Houses* in December 1892 and 'the beginning of modern drama in the English language' –

(to be continued by them that can)

APPENDIX A

[This Will, dated 2nd September 1937, with a Codicil dated 27th November 1940, was granted Probate on 12th February 1944.]

I Charlotte Frances Shaw of 4 Whitehall Court in the County of London Wife of George Bernard Shaw *hereby revoke* all testamentary dispositions heretofore made by me *and declare* this to be my last Will which I make this second day of September One thousand nine hundred and thirty seven.

1. *I desire* to be cremated and that my ashes shall be taken to Ireland and scattered on Irish ground and *I also desire* that no flowers shall be sacrificed, no black clothes worn and no memorial service held at my funeral.
2. *Inasmuch* as I have an English domicile it is my wish and intention that this my Will and any Codicil hereto shall be construed and operate as if I were now and remained until my death domiciled in England.
3. (a) *I appoint* my Husband the said *George Bernard Shaw* and *The National Provincial Bank Limited* (hereinafter called 'the English Bank') to be the *Executors* and General *Trustees* of this my Will and I declare that the English Bank may act as such Executor and Trustee on the terms and conditions and (subject as hereinafter mentioned) with the right of remuneration set forth in the English Bank's Trustee and Executorship Regulations in force at the date hereof.

   (b) As from the date of my death or the death of my said Husband whichever event shall last happen *I appoint The National City Bank Limited* of Number 10 College Green Dublin (hereinafter called 'the Irish Bank') to be the *Special Trustee* of this my Will as respects the ultimate Trust Fund hereinafter mentioned and I *declare* that the Irish Bank may act as such Trustee on the terms and conditions and (subject as hereinafter mentioned) with the right of remuneration set forth in the Irish Bank's Trustee and Executorship Regulations in force at the date hereof and

   (c) *I declare also* that the expression 'my Trustees' shall mean the General Trustees or Trustee for the time being hereof whether original or substituted except where such construction is precluded by the context.
4. *I bequeath* all my 'personal chattels' as defined by Section 55 (1) (X) of the Administration of Estates Act 1925 to my said Husband but if he shall

predecease me then subject to the provisions of Clause 5 hereof to my niece Cecily Charlotte Colthurst.

5.   If at my death I should be possessed of any manuscripts of published or unpublished works or writings, letters, papers or documents of whatever kind relating to or connected with my said Husband George Bernard Shaw or his work (hereinafter called 'my Husband's papers') and bequeathed by him to me under his Will should he predecease me then *I direct* the English Bank to hand over all my Husband's papers to The Public Trustee or other the Executors or Trustees of his Will to be dealt with and held by him or them *Upon the Trusts* declared in the said Will of my said Husband concerning my Husband's papers in all respects as if I had predeceased my said Husband.

6.   *I bequeath* the following legacies free of all duties namely:

To Sidney James Baron Passfield the sum of One thousand pounds.

To John Frederick Leman Whelen the sum of Five hundred pounds.

7.   *I bequeath* the following legacies and annuities free of duties to vest and to commence to be payable on and from the date of the death of the survivor of myself and my said Husband (hereinafter called 'the date of payment') videlicet:

(i) (a) *To* my Gardener Harry Batchelor Higgs the sum of One hundred and fifty pounds and to his Wife Clara the sum of One hundred and fifty pounds but if either of them shall die before the date of payment the legacy of the one so dying shall be payable to the survivor.

(b) *To* the said Harry Batchelor Higgs and Clara Higgs during their joint lives an annuity of Three hundred and twelve pounds payable to them in equal shares of One hundred and fifty six pounds each and after the death of one of them the whole of the said annuity of Three hundred and twelve pounds shall be paid to the survivor of them during his or her life.

(ii) (a) *To* my chauffeur George Frederick Day the sum of One hundred pounds if he shall be living at the date of payment.

(b) *To* the said George Frederick Day during his life and his present Wife after his death if she shall survive him an annuity of One hundred and fifty six pounds.

(iii) *To* Emma Hodgman formerly in my service as housemaid an annuity of Fifty two pounds during her life.

(iv) *To* Kate Hodgman formerly in my service as parlourmaid an annuity of Fifty two pounds during her life.

(v) *To* Mrs Margaret Bilton of 48, Wilman Road Tunbridge Wells Kent an annuity of One hundred and fifty six pounds during her life and to Alice Bilton (daughter of the said Margaret Bilton) after the death of her Mother if the said Alice Bilton shall survive the said Margaret Bilton an annuity of One hundred and four pounds.

8. *The* annuities bequeathed by this my Will or any Codicil hereto are to be payable as and from the date of payment by equal weekly monthly or quarterly payments whichever shall be most convenient to my Trustees and to the respective annuitants the final decision as to the method of payment of the said annuities to rest with my Trustees and the first payments to be made at the expiration of one week month or quarter from the date of payment according to whether the annuities are paid weekly monthly or quarterly.

9. (i) *I declare* that my Trustees may provide for the said annuities by purchasing Government or Insurance Office Annuities or may appropriate and retain a sufficient part of my estate or of the investments representing the same of the nature hereinafter authorised as investments of trust moneys under this my Will as a fund for answering by the annual income thereof the annuities hereinbefore given and the expenses incidental to the payment thereof respectively with power to vary such investments. *And I declare* that if the annual income of the appropriated fund shall at the time of appropriation be sufficient to satisfy the said annuities or such of them as shall for the time being be payable under this my Will such appropriation shall be a complete satisfaction of the trust or direction hereinafter declared to provide for such annuities and that no annuitant shall have any claim against or right to resort to any part of my estate (other than the said appropriated fund) for the payment of his or her annuity and further that if the income of the appropriated fund shall at any time prove insufficient for payment in full of any of the said annuities resort may be had to the capital thereof from time to time to make good such deficiency and the surplus income (if any) of the said fund from time to time remaining after payment of the said annuities shall be applicable as income of the ultimate Trust Fund (hereinafter defined).

(ii) As and when any of the said annuities shall cease the appropriated fund or so much thereof as shall not have been applied in payment of the said annuities or any of them and shall not be required to answer any subsisting annuity shall sink into and form part of the ultimate Trust Fund and until any such annuity shall be provided for in manner aforesaid the same shall be paid out of the income of my residuary estate.

10. *The* foregoing annuities shall in all cases become operative only if the named annuitant shall not have done or suffered anything whereby the

bequeathed annuity or any part of it would through the annuitant's act or default or by operation or process of law or otherwise become vested in some other person or persons and shall continue only until and unless the annuitant shall assign charge or encumber or affect to assign charge or encumber the relevant annuity or any part thereof. And in the event of any of the said annuities not becoming or ceasing to become payable otherwise than by the death of the annuitant my Trustees may at their absolute discretion apply the annuity for the benefit of the annuitant or add it to the income of the ultimate Trust Fund.

11. *I devise* and *bequeath* all the real and personal property whatsoever and wheresoever of or to which I shall be seized possessed or entitled at my death or over which I shall then have a general power of appointment or disposition by Will or of which I shall then be tenant in tail in possession except property otherwise disposed of by this my Will or any Codicil hereto *Unto* my Trustees *Upon the Trusts* and with and subject to the powers and provisions hereinafter declared of and concerning the same that is to say:

12. *Upon Trust* that my Trustees shall sell call in collect and convert into money the said real and personal property at such time or times and in such manner as they shall think fit (but as to reversionary property not until it falls into possession unless it should appear to my Trustees that an earlier sale would be beneficial) with power to postpone the sale calling in or conversion of the whole or any part or parts of the said property including leaseholds or other property of a terminable hazardous or wasting nature during such period as they shall think proper and to retain the same or any part thereof in its present form of investment without being responsible for loss *And I direct* that the income of such of the same premises as for the time being shall remain unsold shall as well during the first year after my death as afterwards be applied as if the same were income arising from investments hereinafter directed to be made of the proceeds of sale thereof and that no reversionary or other property not actually producing income shall be treated as producing income for the purposes of this my Will.

13. *My* Trustees shall out of the moneys to arise from the sale calling in and conversion of or forming part of my said real and personal estate pay my funeral and testamentary expenses (including all estate duty leviable at my death in respect of my residuary estate) and debts and the legacies and annuities given by this my Will and any Codicil hereto and all death duties and other moneys which under or by virtue of any direction or bequest free of duty contained in this my Will or any Codicil hereto are payable out of my general personal estate.

14. *My* Trustees shall at their discretion invest the residue of the said moneys in the names of my Trustees in or upon any of the investments

hereby authorised with power to vary or transpose such investments for or into others of a nature hereby authorised.

15.   *My* Trustees shall stand possessed of the residue of the said moneys and the investments for the time being representing the same and such part of my estate as shall for the time being remain unsold and unconverted (all of which premises are hereinafter referred to as 'the Trust Fund') *Upon the Trusts* following that is to say:

16.   *Upon Trust* to pay the annual income of the Trust Fund to my said Husband if he shall survive me during his life and subject thereto.

17.   *Upon Trust* to raise out of the Trust Fund a legacy of Twenty thousand pounds free of duty (thereinafter called 'Mrs Colthurst's Fund') and to hold the same *Upon Trust* to invest the said legacy in any of the investments hereby authorised and to pay the annual income thereof to my niece Cecily Charlotte Colthurst during her life and after her death my Trustees shall hold Mrs Colthurst's Fund *Upon Trust* for such of them her two daughters Mary Penelope Hamilton and Shournagh Dorothy Combe as shall survive me and if both then in equal shares absolutely but if either of my said nieces shall predecease me leaving a child or children who shall survive me and attain the age of twenty one years such child or children shall take by substitution if more than one in equal shares as tenants in common the share of and in Mrs Colthurst's Fund which such niece would have taken if she had survived me *And* subject to the trusts aforesaid Mrs Colthurst's Fund shall fall into and form part of the ultimate Trust Fund hereinafter mentioned.

18.   *Subject* to the trusts aforesaid and to the powers hereby or by law conferred upon my Trustees and to any and every exercise of such respective powers my Trustees shall stand possessed of the Trust Fund or the residue thereof which premises and the property for the time being representing the same are in this my Will for brevity called 'the Ultimate Trust Fund' *Upon Trust* as soon as conveniently may be after my death or the death of my Husband whichever event shall last happen to transfer the same to and vest the same in the Irish bank.

19.   (i)   *Whereas:*

      (a) I am desirous of promoting and encouraging in Ireland the bringing of the masterpieces of fine art within the reach of the Irish people of all classes so that they may have increased opportunity of studying such masterpieces and of acquiring a fuller and wider knowledge thereof, and

      (b) In the course of a long life I have had many opportunities of observing the extent to which the most highly instructed and capable persons have their efficiency defeated and their influence limited for want of any organised instruction and training for the personal contacts whether with individuals or popular audiences without which their knowledge is incommunicable (except through books) and how the authority which their abilities should give them is made derisory by their awkward manners and how their employment in positions for which they have valuable qualifications is made socially impossible by vulgarities of speech and other defects as easily corrigible by teaching and training as simple illiteracy and whereas my experience and observation have convinced me that the lack of such training produces not only much social friction but grave pathological results which seem quite unconnected with it and that social intercourse is a fine art with a technique which everybody can and should acquire.

(ii) *Now* with a view to furthering and carrying out the objects which I have at heart *I hereby declare* that the Irish Bank shall stand possessed of the Ultimate Trust Fund as and when so transferred to and vested in the Irish Bank *Upon the Trusts* and with and subject to the powers and provision following that is to say:

(a) The Irish Bank may either allow the same or any part or parts thereof respectively to remain as actually invested so long as the Irish Bank shall think fit or may at any time or times at the discretion of the Irish Bank sell call in or convert into money the same or any part thereof and at the like discretion invest the moneys produced thereby and any other capital moneys which may be received by the Irish Bank in respect of the Ultimate Trust Fund in the name of the Irish Bank in or upon any investments or investment hereby authorised with power at such discretion as aforesaid to vary or transpose any investments for or into another or others of any nature hereby authorised.

(b) The Irish Bank shall pay or apply the net income of the Ultimate Trust Fund in perpetuity to in or towards all or any one or more of the following objects and in such proportions and in such manner as the Irish Bank shall in its absolute discretion from time to time think fit that is to say:

(c) The making of grants contributions and payments to any foundation corporate body institution association or fund now existing or hereafter coming into existence within the special period hereinafter defined having for its object the bringing of the masterpieces of fine art within the reach of the people of Ireland of all classes in their own country provided that no such foundation corporate body institution association or fund shall be eligible as an object of this trust if:

(i) It is not of a public character or

(ii) In the case of a foundation corporate body institution or association it is at liberty to pay or distribute any profits to or among any of its members subscribers contributors or bene-factors or the fund or any part thereof or any income there-from may be so paid or applied or

(iii) Any of the members subscribers contributors or benefactors would have any right to participate in the assets or in the fund in the event of its dissolution or distribution.

(d) The teaching promotion and encouragement in Ireland of self control, elocution, oratory, deportment, the arts of personal con-tact, of social intercourse, and the other arts of public, private, professional and business life.

(e) The establishment and endowment within the special period either solely or jointly with any person or persons or any other corporation of any educational institution or any Chair or Read-ership in any University College or Educational Institution now existing or coming into existence within the special period in Ireland for the purpose of giving instruction in or promoting the study by the general public of the subjects mentioned in this Clause 19 or any of them Provided that no such College or Educational Institution has for its sole object the exclusive or complete training in any single profession or calling.

(iii) *I declare* that for the purpose of this my Will the expression 'master-pieces of fine art' means and includes works of the highest class in the fields of orchestral and classical music painting sculpture fine printing and literature produced or originating not in any one Country exclus-ively but in any Country in the world and by or among people in any age period or date whether ancient or modern.

20. *I declare* that the expression 'the special period' hereinbefore referred to shall mean the lives of the issue now living of his late Majesty King George the Fifth and the life of the survivor of them and twenty one years after the death of the survivor of them.

21. *Notwithstanding* anything herein contained I empower the Irish Bank for any of the foregoing purposes or objects in its absolute discretion to expend or lay out the capital of the Ultimate Trust Fund or any part thereof in paying or transferring the same to the Trustees or other Governing Body of any such foundation corporate body institution association fund edu-cational institution (whether or not established by the Irish Bank under the power in that behalf hereinbefore contained) University or College as hereinbefore mentioned either absolutely or by way of loan and if by way of loan either at such rate of interest as the Irish Bank shall think fit or without charging any interest.

22.   *Without* prejudice to the right of the Irish Bank to employ and pay any Secretary Clerk or other administrative officer or officers (whether a member or members of its Staff or not) for the purpose of administering the foregoing trusts of the Ultimate Trust Fund if the Irish Bank shall deem it necessary or desirable so to do it is my desire that the moneys directed to be paid or applied under such foregoing trusts shall be used directly for the promotion of the objects therein referred to and shall not be expended for the erection of new buildings the maintenance of buildings or for the upkeep of any establishment or the maintenance of any subordinate Staff employed in connection with the said objects or in any manner ancillary to the main objects but notwithstanding this indication of my wishes I *give* the Irish Bank uncontrolled discretion as to the manner in which such moneys shall be expended or applied for or towards any or all of the above objects.

23.   *The* expression 'Ireland' wherever used in this my Will shall denote the existing Irish Free State and any other future extension of it that may take place.

24.   *All* moneys liable to be invested under this my Will may be invested in or upon any Stocks funds or securities of or guaranteed by the Government of the United Kingdom of Great Britain and Northern Ireland or India or any British Colony or Dependency (including therein any Dominion Commonwealth Union or Mandated Territory forming part of the British Empire or any Province or State having a separate local legislature and forming part thereof respectively and including Ireland) or any Foreign State or in or upon the Stocks Shares Bonds Debentures Securities or Investments of any Company or of any Municipal or other Corporation Local Board or Public Body in the United Kingdom as aforesaid or British Colony or Dependency as aforesaid or in the purchase or on mortgage (whether contributory or otherwise) of any real or leasehold property in the United Kingdom as aforesaid or in Ireland.

25. (a) The aforesaid right of the English Bank to remuneration shall not include the right to any withdrawal fee in respect of the Ultimate Trust Fund or any part thereof.

(b) The aforesaid right of the Irish Bank to remuneration shall be varied in that the Irish Bank shall in lieu of the usual income fee be entitled to an income fee at the rate of Five pounds per centum on the gross income before deduction of income tax or any other outgoings with a minimum yearly income fee of One hundred and fifty pounds in addition to such payment (if any) as it shall make to any Secretary Clerk or other administrative officer or officers in accordance with the authority hereinbefore given.

26.   *I suggest* that on any occasion on which the services of a Solicitor may be

required it will be advisable to resort to the firm of Barrington & Son of Dublin for Irish business and for other than Irish business the firm of Lawrence, Graham & Company of London as these firms are conversant with my affairs but without prejudice to the right of any Bank being at the time an Executor or Trustee hereof to consult any other Solicitor in any case in which it shall think it proper so to do.

In witness whereof I have hereunto set my hand the day and year first above written

Signed by the above named Testatrix
Charlotte Frances Shaw as and for her last Will in the presence of us present at the same time who in her presence and at her request and in the presence of each other have hereunto subscribed our names as witnesses

Charlotte Frances Shaw

E. W. Wykes
  New Square
  Lincoln's Inn
Solicitor

[Signature indecipherable] MRCS LRCP
  50 York Mansions
  SW11
Medical Practitioner

I, CHARLOTTE FRANCES SHAW of 4, Whitehall Court in the County of London, wife of George Bernard Shaw DECLARE this to be a Codicil to my Will which bears date the second day of September One thousand nine hundred and thirty-seven.

1. I BEQUEATH the letters which were written to me by Colonel T.E. Lawrence and which are at present in safe custody at the British Museum to the British Museum absolutely.

2. I BEQUEATH the sum of One hundred pounds to ROBERT STUD-MAN free of duty who is employed at 4, Whitehall Court and attending to me and Fifty pounds to MAGGIE CASHIN free of duty who is in my service and I declare that the said legacies shall be paid to them whether or not he or she shall

be at 4, Whitehall Court and attending to me or in my service at the date of my death.

3. IN all other respects I confirm my said Will IN WITNESS whereof I have hereunto set my hand this twenty seventh day of November One thousand nine hundred and forty.

SIGNED by the above-named Testatrix
in our presence by us in her presence
and in that of each other

Charlotte Frances Shaw

Blanche E. Patch
    Onslow Court Hotel
    Queen's Gate
    SW7
Spinster

Clara Rebecca Higgs
    Ayot St Lawrence Welwyn Herts
Housekeeper

APPENDIX B

BERNARD SHAW'S
LAST WILL AND TESTAMENT

[This Will, dated 12th June, 1950, was granted Probate on 20th March, 1951.]

This is the Last Will and Testament of me George Bernard Shaw of 4 Whitehall Court in the County of London and of Ayot Saint Lawrence in the County of Herts   Author

1. I revoke all Wills and testamentary dispositions heretofore made by me.

2. I appoint the Public Trustee as the sole Executor and Trustee of this my Will who is hereinafter referred to as 'my Trustee.'

3. I desire that my dead body shall be cremated and its ashes inseparably mixed with those of my late wife now in the custody of the Golders Green Crematorium and in this condition inurned or scattered in the garden of the house in Ayot Saint Lawrence where we lived together for thirty five years unless some other disposal of them should be in the opinion of my Trustee more eligible. Personally I prefer the garden to the cloister.

4. As my religious convictions and scientific views cannot at present be more specifically defined than as those of a believer in Creative Evolution I desire that no public monument or work of art or inscription or sermon or ritual service commemorating me shall suggest that I accepted the tenets peculiar to any established Church or denomination [*sic*] nor take the form of a cross or any other instrument of torture or symbol of blood sacrifice.

5. I bequeath my copyrights performing rights filming rights television rights and all cognate rights now in existence or hereafter to be created with the manuscripts typescripts and other documents in which I have such rights to my Trustee Upon trust to apply the proceeds resulting from the exploitation of such rights or the sale or other lucrative use of such documents as income of my estate.

6. I bequeath all papers and documents in my possession in which I have no copyright and which belong to me as material objects only to my Trustee to be examined as soon as conveniently after my death and divided as nearly as may be into sections as follows:—
Section A. Papers (if any) concerning my late wife's family or affairs.

Section B. Old Diaries account books Bank passbooks paid cheques and their counterfoils expired agreements box office returns and other records of my business operations and personal and domestic expenditure capable of being used by economic or legal historians or by biographers seeking documentary evidence as to prices and practices during the period covered by my lifetime.

Section C. Such letters and documents as might be worth preserving in a public collection such as that of the British Museum.

Section D. All documents needed for the administration of my estate and the carrying out of the provisions of this my Will.

Section E. Uninteresting documents of no use except as waste paper.

I bequeath the contents of these sections to my Trustee with the suggestion that the contents of Section A (if any) be presented to my late wife's niece Mrs Cecily Charlotte Colthurst or should she predecease me to such surviving relative of hers as my Trustee may select; that the contents of Section B be offered to the British Library of Political Science in Clare Market London for the purpose indicated and those of Section C to the British Museum or failing acceptance to any other suitable public collection whilst the contents of Sections D and E can be retained or destroyed by my Trustee as may be expedient. And I declare that if any doubt or disputes should arise as to which papers shall be thus dealt with the question shall be settled by my Trustee whose decision shall be final Provided Always that my Trustee shall retain all or any of the aforesaid papers and documents for such period as shall in his opinion be desirable.

7. I declare that my Trustee shall manage and deal with my author's rights with all the powers in that behalf of an absolute owner (subject as hereinafter provided) for so long as may prove necessary or expedient during a period ending at the expiration of twenty years from the day of the death of the last survivor of all the lineal descendants of His late Majesty King George the Fifth who shall be living at the time of my death (hereinafter called 'the Special period') bearing in mind that the licensing of theatrical performances and especially of cinematographic exhibitions and the like with the collection of royalties thereon will be a principal source of revenue besides continuing my practice in England of manufacturing my literary works at the cost of my estate and causing copies thereof to be sold on commission by a Publisher and shall make such other arrangements with Publishers and others as my Trustee shall think fit Provided always that my Trustee shall not sell assign or alienate such copyrights and other rights or any of them and shall not grant any licence or enter into any agreement or other arrangement in respect of the said copyrights and other rights or any of them which shall irrevocably bind or affect the same for a period

exceeding five years (unless with power of revocation) at any one time calculated from the date of the execution of such licence agreement or arrangement but with power to renew or re-grant the same for any period not exceeding the aforesaid period and so on from time to time And I further declare that my Trustee shall not in dealing with any such rights be bound by commercial considerations exclusively it being my desire that he shall give due weight to artistic and public and human considerations to the best of his judgment and counsel.

8. I desire that my Trustee shall do all things and make out of my estate all payments necessary to preserve my aforesaid copyrights or any of them and to procure any renewal of the same that can be obtained And I authorise him to make such payments accordingly And for the guidance of my Trustee I record that with regard to my copyrights in the United States of America (which are of considerable value) the same do not continue automatically for a period of fifty years from the author's death (as in England and other countries) but continue for a period of twenty eight years only from the date of first publication with a right of renewal for a further period of twenty eight years upon application being made and registered within one year prior to the expiration of the first term.

9. I direct my Trustee without charging any payment to authorise Mrs Stella Mervyn Beech now residing at 122 Sussex Gardens in the County of London W.2 daughter of the late eminent actress professionally known as Mrs Patrick Campbell to print and publish after my death all or any of the letters written by me to the said eminent actress and in the event of Mrs Beech's death before such publication to give such authority (which is a permission and not an assignment of copyright) to Mrs Patrick Campbell's grandson Patrick Beech and without imposing any trust I desire that the proceeds of such publication should be reserved as far as possible by Mrs Beech or Patrick Beech for the secondary education of Mrs Campbell's grandchildren and their children (such being her own wish) and any legacy duty payable by reason of such authority being given shall be paid out of my estate.

10. Whereas I possess a bust of myself in white marble by the eminent Hungarian sculptor Sigismund Strobl and now in the custody of the London County Council I bequeath it to the as yet unbuilt Shakespeare Memorial National Theatre in London and I direct my Trustee to leave the said bust in the said custody until the opening of the said National Theatre.

11. Whereas certain portraits of myself in painting or sculpture are at present in public galleries or institutions as for example the marble bust by Rodin in the Dublin Municipal Gallery a painting by Augustus John in the

Fitzwilliam Museum in Cambridge a bust in bronze by Paul Troubetskoy in the National Gallery of British Art at Millbank in London (known also as The Tate Gallery) and an earlier bronze by the same sculptor in the Foyer of the Theatre Guild at 245 West 52nd Street in New York City I bequeath all of them and any others that may be in the like circumstances at my death to the several institutions in whose custody they stand save that in the case of the said Theatre Guild which is not in its nature a permanent institution I direct that on the Guild's dissolution or the winding up of its business from any cause during the special period the bust shall pass to the Metropolitan Museum in New York City or failing its acceptance for immediate or future exhibition in that institution to the next most eligible (in my Trustee's opinion) American public collection willing to accept it.

12. I bequeath absolutely the Crayon drawing of the late Harley Granville-Barker by John Singer Sargent to the Trustees for the time being of the National Portrait Gallery in London in whose custody it now is.

13. I bequeath to the National Trust all that is mine of the furniture cars and other contents except my cars and their appurtenances of the house garage and garden and grounds in the village of Ayot Saint Lawrence ordnance mapped as 'Shaw's Corner' now the property of the said National Trust to be preserved as objects of memorial or artistic interest or disposed of or held in reserve for the benefit of the said premises or the said village as to the said Trust may in its judgment seem advisable.

14. Whereas it has been my custom to allow the Actors' Orphanage to receive and retain fees collected by the Collection Bureau of the Incorporated Society of Authors Playwrights and Composers for performance in the United Kingdom of my play entitled 'Passion Poison and Petrifaction' and I desire that such arrangement shall be continued Now I hereby direct my Trustee to continue such arrangement accordingly and to permit and authorise the performance (but without expense to my estate) of my aforesaid play at any time on the request of the Secretary of the aforesaid Society or of the aforesaid Orphanage and for the benefit thereof and to allow the aforesaid Society to continue to collect all fees in respect of the aforesaid play and pay the same to the aforesaid Orphanage for the benefit thereof and if any such fees as aforesaid shall come to the hands of my Trustee then my Trustee shall hold the same upon trust for such Orphanage absolutely And I declare that the receipt of the Secretary Treasurer or other officer of the aforesaid Society or of the aforesaid Orphanage for any such fees as aforesaid shall be a sufficient discharge for the same and that any legacy duty payable in respect of the same shall be borne by the said Orphanage.

15. I authorise the Fabian Society of London so long as it shall remain an avowedly Socialistic Society and after it shall have ceased so to be if and whilst such avowal shall be contrary to law to print and publish for the benefit of such Society and its Cause all writing [*sic*] of mine which are or shall be at the time of my death included or with my consent about to be included amongst its publications and I direct my Trustee if necessary to grant to such Society such license as will give effect completely or as far as possible to the provisions of this Clause which however must not be construed as giving the said Society any sole or exclusive property in the copyrights concerned and any legacy duty payable by reason of such license being given shall be borne by the said Society.

16. I empower my Trustee to procure all necessary assistance and expert advice legal artistic literary or other for the discharge of his relevant functions and to pay its cost out of my estate.

17. Provided always And I declare that as my fashion of literary composition often obliges me to make my first draft without full and final regard to temperance of expression generosity or justice to individuals accuracy of history or public propriety generally and to remedy this imperfection by later corrections it is my wish and I charge my Trustee and all others under whose eyes any of my literary works and documents may pass not to publish or quote or suffer to be published or quoted any edition or extracts from my works in which any earlier text shall be substituted either wholly or partly for the text as contained in the printed volumes finally passed by me for press except in the case of texts which I may be prevented by death or disablement from so passing And further that in any critical or biographical notes that may from good reasons make public any passages written by me but subsequently altered or discarded heed be taken both to the credit and the feelings of any surviving person alluded to therein but no suppressions need be made for the purpose of whitewashing my own character or conduct.

18. I bequeath to every indoor and outdoor servant or labourer including charwoman chauffeur and gardener (hereinafter respectively referred to as such servant) of mine (other than any such as may be entitled to an annuity or pension under the provisions of the following clauses of this my Will) who shall be in the exclusive employ or in the case of my residing in a service flat the daily service of me at the time of my death and shall then have been in such employ for a continuous or virtually continuous period (that is to say only interrupted by illness or the like or military service and not by a formal discharge) of not less than seven years a sum equal to one year's wages or periodical gratuity of such servant and to every such servant

of mine (other than as aforesaid) who shall be in the exclusive employ of me at the time of my death and shall then have been in my employ for a period of less than seven years but for a continuous or virtually continuous period of not less than three years a sum equal to six months' wages or periodical gratuity of such servant and to every such servant of mine (other than as aforesaid) who shall be in the exclusive employ of me at the time of my death and shall then have been in such employ for a period of less than three years a sum equal to three months' wages or periodical gratuity of such servant all such bequests as aforesaid to be in addition to any wages that may be or become legally due to any such servant as aforesaid Provided always And I further declare that whether the foregoing bequests shall become operative or not my Trustee shall have absolute power to act reasonably and generously in the case of any servant of mine or of my late wife who in the opinion of my Trustee is not sufficiently dealt with under the provisions hereinbefore made and accordingly to make to any such servant any such payment or additional payment out of my Estate as my Trustee shall in his discretion think desirable but without imposing any obligation upon him to make any such payment.

19. I declare that every annuity hereinafter or by any Codicil hereto bequeathed is bequeathed subject to the provisions relating to annuities hereinafter contained.

20. I declare that if at the time of my death any person or persons who shall not then be in my employ but shall have formerly been in the employ of me or of my late wife and who shall not otherwise become entitled to any benefit under this my Will and shall be in receipt of a pension or allowance from me then I bequeath to such person or persons an Annuity equal in amount to the amount of such pension or allowance of which such former servant shall be then in receipt.

21. I bequeath to my retired gardener Harry Batchelor Higgs an annuity of One hundred and fifty six pounds and I direct my Trustee to see to it that the monument I have had erected in Windlesham Cemetery to him and his late wife shall on his death at the cost of my estate have its inscription completed and thereafter be cared for by the Cemetery authorities in consideration of an appropriate capital sum.

22. I bequeath to Emma Hodgman formerly in my service as Housemaid and now or lately resident at 130 Windmill Road in Gillingham Kent an annuity of Fifty two pounds.

23. I bequeath to Mrs Margaret Bilton now or lately residing at 48 Wilmer Road Tunbridge Wells and formerly in my service as housekeeper an

annuity of One hundred and fifty six pounds to be continued after her death to her daughter Alice Bilton if surviving and on the respective deaths of the said Margaret Bilton and the said Alice Bilton I direct my Trustee to pay or apply for the benefit of the survivor of them or to such other person or persons and in such manner as he shall in his discretion think fit a sum of Twenty five pounds out of the capital of my Residuary Estate for or towards the funeral expenses incurred consequent on their respective deaths.

24. Whereas the annuities hereby bequeathed to Harry Batchelor [The surname, Higgs, was inadvertently omitted by the calligrapher.] Frederick William Day and Margaret Day Mrs Margaret Bilton and Alice Bilton and Emma Hodgman are provided for as from my death by the Will of my late wife Charlotte Frances Shaw my bequests to them herein shall be subject to such reductions and increases as may bring their benefits to the same level as if only one Will and that the most favourable to them shall come into force at my decease.

25. I bequeath to Mrs Georgina Musters the daughter of my mother's half sister Arabella Gillmore an annuity of Three hundred and sixty five pounds.

26. I bequeath to Eames Bagenal Rogers now or lately residing at 1249 Yale Street Santa Monica California the son of my mother's late half-sister Charlotte Rogers and to his wife after his death if she shall survive him an annuity of Fifty two pounds.

27. I bequeath to Georgina Meredith now residing at 34 Barrow Street in the City of Dublin daughter of my mother's late half-sister Charlotte Rogers an annuity of Fifty two pounds.

28. I bequeath to Ethel Gordon Walters at present residing at 34 Queens Gardens in the County of London W.1 daughter of my first cousin the late James Cockaigne Shaw an annuity of Two hundred and thirty four pounds.

29. I bequeath to my former housemaid Mrs Ronald Smith (born Margaret Cashin) a deferred annuity of Fifty two pounds a year should she survive or be separated from her husband Ronald Smith or a later husband if any.

30. I bequeath to my chauffeur and gardener Frederick William Day and his Wife Margaret Day jointly an annuity of One hundred and fifty six pounds to be continued in full to the survivor of them.

31. I bequeath to Eva Maria Schneider now residing at 196 Rivermead Court Hurlingham London S.W.6 an annuity of One hundred and twenty pounds in remembrance of her devoted services to my late sister Lucy.

32. I bequeath to my Secretary Blanche Patch Spinster an annuity of Five hundred pounds.

33. The following provisions shall apply to all annuities hereby or by any Codicil hereto bequeathed—

   (1) The bequest of an annuity shall become operative only if the named annuitant shall not at my death have done or suffered anything whereby the bequeathed annuity or any part of it would become vested in or payable to some other person or persons and shall continue only until the annuitant shall become bankrupt or assign or charge the said annuity or any part thereof or do or suffer anything whereby the said annuity or any part thereof would become vested in or payable to any other person and in the event of any annuity not becoming or ceasing to become payable by the effect of this subclause my Trustee may at his absolute discretion during the rest of the life of the annuitant apply out of the income of my residuary trust funds hereinafter defined any sums not exceeding in any year the amount of the relevant annuity for the benefit of the annuitant and for the purposes of sub-clause (3) of this clause any sums which my Trustee decides to apply as aforesaid in any year shall be treated as if the aggregate of the same was an annuity.

   (2) Every annuity shall be payable by equal quarterly payments payable in advance the first payment to become payable as at my death and to be paid as soon thereafter as my Trustee is in a position to pay the same.

   (3) Every annuity shall unless and until a sum shall have been appropriated to provide for the same as hereinafter authorised or until the expiration of twenty one years from my death or the previous cesser whether partial or complete of the trust of the balance of the income of my Residuary Trust Funds hereinafter contained be payable only out of the income of my Residuary Trust Funds in each year from my death available for the payment thereof and if the income of my Residuary Trust Funds shall be insufficient to pay the said annuities in full the annuitant shall be entitled to be paid any capital sum in satisfaction of his or her annuity as a legacy but the said annuity shall abate pro rata for such period and to such an extent as shall be necessary having regard to the insufficiency of such income as aforesaid but if at the end of any year from my death there should be income available (after paying the full amounts of the said annuities for the time being payable for that year) to pay the amounts or part of the amounts by which the annuities then still payable had previously abated my Trustee shall out of such income pay the said amounts or such parts of the said amounts and rateably in proportion to such last mentioned annuities as such income shall be sufficient to satisfy. Upon the expiration of twenty one years

from my death or the cesser whether partial or complete of the said trust of the balance of the said income the annuities then subsisting if not then provided for under sub-clause (4) hereof and any amounts by which such annuities had previously abated if not made good shall be a charge on the capital of my Residuary Trust Funds.

(4) My Trustee may in his discretion at any time provide for the payment of the annuities for the time being subsisting by appropriating and retaining out of my Residuary Trust Funds and investing in the name of my Trustee in any of the investments hereinafter authorised (with power for my Trustee to vary or transpose such investments for others hereby authorised) such a sum as when so invested shall at the time of investment be sufficient by means of the income thereof to pay the said annuities And I declare that such appropriation as aforesaid shall be complete provision for such annuities and that in case the income of the appropriated fund shall at any time prove insufficient for payment in full of such annuities resort may be had to the capital thereof from time to time to make good such deficiency and the surplus (if any) of the income of the said fund from time to time remaining after payment of such annuities shall form part of the income of my Residuary Trust Funds And I declare that as and when any annuity provided for by means of the appropriated fund as aforesaid shall cease to be payable so much of the appropriated fund as my Trustee shall not think it necessary to retain to answer any remaining annuities shall revert to the capital of my Residuary Trust Funds.

(5) My Trustee shall have power if in his absolute discretion he thinks fit during the lives or life of any of the annuitants out of the income of my Residuary Trust Funds in any year not required for payment of such of the annuities as shall for the time being be payable or if he thinks fit out of the capital of my Residuary Trust Funds to make such additional payment to the annuitants for the time being living as in his opinion may be required to make good to such annuitants any decrease in the values of their annuities which shall be due to an increase [sic] [this should read 'decrease'] in the purchasing power of the £ sterling after the date of this my Will.

34. I declare that all legacies (whether pecuniary or specific) and annuities bequeathed by this my Will or any Codicil shall be paid without deduction of legacy duty or any other duties payable in respect of the same and that the said duties including any duty chargeable by reason of an annuity arising on or being increased by the death of any annuitant shall be paid out of my real and personal estate hereinafter devised and bequeathed by way of residue.

35. I devise and bequeath all my real and personal estate not otherwise

specifically disposed of by this my Will or any Codicil hereto and all property over which I have general power of appointment unto my Trustee Upon trust that my Trustee shall (subject to the power of postponing the sale and conversion thereof hereinafter contained) sell my real estate and sell call in or otherwise convert into money as much as may be needed of my personal estate (other than any copyrights which as provided by Clause 7 of this my Will are not to be sold) to increase the ready monies of which I may be possessed at my death to an amount sufficient to pay my funeral and testamentary expenses and debts estate duty legacy duty and all the duties payable on my death in respect of my estate or the bequests hereby made free of duty (other than testamentary expenses) and the legacies bequeathed by this my Will or any Codicil hereto or to make such other payments or investments or change of investments as in his opinion shall be advisable in the interest of my estate and shall invest the residue of such monies in manner hereinafter authorised And shall stand possessed of the said residuary trust moneys and the investments for the time being representing the same and all other investments for the time being forming part of my residuary estate (herein called my Residuary Trust Funds) and the annual income thereof Upon the trusts hereby declared of and concerning the same.

(1) To institute and finance a series of inquiries to ascertain or estimate as far as possible the following statistics (*a*) the number of extant persons who speak the English language and write it by the established and official alphabet of 26 letters (hereinafter called Dr. Johnson's Alphabet) (*b*) how much time could be saved per individual scribe by the substitution for the said Alphabet of an Alphabet containing at least 40 letters (hereinafter called the Proposed British Alphabet) enabling the said language to be written without indicating single sounds by groups of letters or by diacritical marks instead of by one symbol for each sound (*c*) how many of these persons are engaged in writing or printing English at any and every moment in the world; (*d*) on these factors to estimate the time and labour wasted by our lack of at least 14 unequivocal single symbols; (*e*) to add where possible to the estimates of time lost or saved by the difference between Dr. Johnson's Alphabet and the Proposed British Alphabet estimates of the loss of income in British and American currency. The enquiry must be confined strictly to the statistical and mathematical problems to be solved without regard to the views of professional and amateur phoneticians, etymologists, Spelling Reformers, patentees of universal languages, inventors of shorthand codes for verbatim reporting or rival alphabets, teachers of the established orthography, disputants about pronunciation, or any of the irreconcilables whose wranglings have overlooked and confused

the single issue of labour saving and made change impossible during the last hundred years. The inquiry must not imply any approval or disapproval of the Proposed British Alphabet by the inquirers or by my Trustee.

(2) To employ a phonetic expert to transliterate my play entitled 'Androcles & the Lion' into the Proposed British Alphabet assuming the pronunciation to resemble that recorded of His Majesty our late King George V. and sometimes described as Northern English.

(3) To employ an artist-calligrapher to fair-copy the transliteration for reproduction by lithography photography or any other method that may serve in the absence of printers' types.

(4) To advertise and publish the transliteration with the original Dr. Johnson's lettering opposite the transliteration page by page and a glossary of the two alphabets at the end and to present copies to public libraries in the British Isles, the British Commonwealth, the American States North and South and to national libraries everywhere in that order.

36. I desire my Trustee to bear in mind that the Proposed British Alphabet does not pretend to be exhaustive as it contains only sixteen vowels whereas by infinitesimal movements of the tongue countless different vowels can be produced all of them in use among speakers of English who utter the same vowels no oftener than they make the same finger prints. Nevertheless they can understand one another's speech and writing sufficiently to converse and correspond: for instance, a graduate of Trinity College Dublin has no difficulty in understanding a graduate of Oxford University when one says that 'the sun rohze,' and the other 'the san raheoze' nor are either of them puzzled when a peasant calls his childhood his 'chawldid.' For a university graduate calls my native country Awlind.

37. It is possible that the Ministry of Education may institute the inquiry and adopt the Proposed British Alphabet to be taught in the schools it controls in which event subsection 1 of Clause 35 foregoing and its relevant sequels will be contraindicated as superfluous and Clause 40 come into operation accordingly but the adoption must be exact and no account taken of the numerous alternative spelling Reforms now advocated or hereafter proposed.

38. I hereby devise and bequeath the balance of the income of my Residuary Trust Funds not required during the period of twenty one years after my death to pay the annuities hereby or by any Codicil hereto bequeathed or for any other purpose upon which income of my Residuary Trust Funds may under the trusts hereinbefore contained be applicable Upon trust

during the special period but subject to cesser as hereinafter provided To apply the same as follows:—

A. To remunerate the services and defray the expenses incidental to these proceedings and generally to the launching advertising and propaganda of the said British Alphabet.

B. To acquire by employment purchase or otherwise the copyrights and patents (if any) created by or involved in the designing and manufacture of the said Alphabet or the publication of the works printed in it without exploiting the said rights or for commercial profit.

C. To wind-up the enterprise when the aforesaid steps have been taken or if and when its official adoption or general vogue shall make further recourse to my estate and action on the part of my Trustee in respect of this charitable Trust superfluous.

39. Pending the operation of the foregoing clause I direct that my Trustee shall for the said period of twenty one years from my death accumulate the said balance of the income of my Residuary Trust Funds in the way of compound interest by investing the same and the resulting income thereof from time to time in any investment in which my Residuary Trust Funds are authorised to be invested.

40. Subject to the trusts hereinbefore declared of my Residuary Trust Funds and the income thereof or if and so far as such trusts shall fail through judicial decision or any other cause beyond my Trustee's control my Trustee shall stand possessed of my Residuary Trust Funds and the income thereof but subject to a charge on the capital as well as the income thereof for payment of such of the annuities hereby bequeathed as shall be subsisting Upon trust as to one third thereof for the Trustees of the British Museum in acknowledgment of the incalculable value to me of my daily resort to the Reading Room of that Institution at the beginning of my career as to one third of the same Upon trust for the National Gallery of Ireland and as to the remaining one third of the same Upon trust for the Royal Academy of Dramatic Art at 61 Gower Street in the County of London and should any of these three institutions be permanently closed at the date when the trust to accumulate the said balance of income of my Residuary Trust Funds shall cease the others or other shall succeed to its share and if more than one equally.

41. I authorise my Trustee to postpone for such period as he shall in his discretion think fit the sale and conversion of all or any part of my real and personal estate hereinbefore devised and bequeathed in trust for sale and conversion notwithstanding the same may be of a perishable or wearing out nature (but if any part of my estate shall be of a reversionary nature the

same shall not be sold or converted into money until it falls into possession unless my Trustee shall think it probable that a loss will arise to my estate by postponing the sale and conversion thereof) and to retain any stocks shares or securities of which I may be possessed at my death whether fully paid up or not (but my real estate shall be impressed with the quality of personal estate from the time of my death) And I declare that the net income arising from any part of my real or personal estate previous to the sale or conversion thereof shall as well during the first year after my death as afterwards be applied in the same manner as if the same were income arising from such investments as are by this my Will authorised but that no reversionary or other property forming part of my estate not actually producing income shall be treated as producing income.

42. Should my Trustee have occasion to realise any of my investments in the shares and loan stocks of Friendly Societies not quoted on the Stock Exchange and therefore often sold by Executors and others at less than their value I direct my Trustee not to dispose of them without first offering them to the Directors of the said Societies they being commonly ready to liquidate such stocks at their face value.

43. I declare that my Trustee shall be at liberty to grant time or other indulgence to any debtor in respect of any unsecured personal loans made by me and (in particular when the loan has not in his judgment been a matter of business) to forego payment of and absolutely release all or any part of the amount of any such debts or loan without being answerable for any loss which may thereby arise and with regard to any such debts owing to me or claims I may have against any person or persons I express it to be my wish that my Trustee shall in the exercise of the aforesaid power deal kindly or leniently with all such debtors or other person or persons where a strict observation of the law would involve manifest injustice hardship or meanness (but no distinction in this respect is to be made in favour of my relatives as distinguished from other persons) And I also declare that certain bequests I have made in former Wills in favour of various persons I have now omitted to make not on account of any change of feeling on my part towards them but because deaths marriages and change of circumstances have rendered such bequests unnecessary and I also record my regret that my means are not sufficient to provide for material pledges of my regard for the many friends who as colleagues in the Socialistic movement or as artists co-operating with me in the performance of my plays or otherwise have not only made my career possible but hallowed it with kindly human relations.

44. I declare that all monies liable to be invested under my Will may be invested

in any investment or securities for the time being authorised by law for the investment of trust funds.

45. I authorise my Trustee to apportion as my Trustee shall think fit among the trust premises any charges deductions or outgoings whatsoever and to determine whether any money shall for the purpose of this my Will be considered annual income or not and the power of appropriation conferred by the administration of Estates Act 1925 shall be exercisable by my Trustee whether acting as personal representative or trustee and without any of the consents made requisite by that Act.

46. I declare that the Executor and Trustee for the time being of this my Will may instead of acting personally employ and pay a Solicitor Accountant Agent Literary Executor Bibliographer or any other person or persons to transact any business or do any act required to be done in connection with the administration of my estate or the trusts hereby declared including the receipt and payment of money and the keeping and preparation of books and accounts And I express it to be my wish (but without imposing any obligation) that my present English Solicitors the firm of J. N. Mason & Co of 41–44 Temple Chambers in the City of London my American Attorneys the firm of Stern & Reubens of 1 East 45th Street in New York City my Accountant Walter Smee now practising at 22 Shaftesbury Avenue West Central London, my British Publishers Messrs Constable & Co of 10 Orange Street in the County of London my Printers Messrs R. & R. Clark of Brandon Street Edinburgh, my present Secretary Blanche Patch, my Bibliographer Fritz Erwin Loewenstein Doctor of Philosophy and Founder of the London Shaw Society (now residing at Torca Cottage in Saint Albans) whose knowledge of my literary affairs and interest in my reputation qualify him exceptionally for such employment shall be consulted and employed by my Executor and Trustee whenever their assistance may be desirable and available and that the Incorporated Society of Authors Playwrights and Composers shall continue to be employed as my Theatrical Agents on the special conditions now established between us. To this I add that my country Solicitor Ivo L. Currall of 2 Gordon Chambers 1 Upper George Street Luton in the County of Bedford is also familiar with my local affairs.

47. Having been born a British subject in Ireland in 1856 subsequently registered as a citizen of Eire and finally privileged to remain a British subject by the Home Secretary's letter dated the twenty seventh day of June One thousand nine hundred and forty nine I declare that my domicile of choice is English and desire that my Will be construed and take effect according to English law.

In Witness whereof I have hereunto to set my hand to this and the thirteen preceding sheets of paper this twelfth day of June One thousand nine hundred and fifty.

Signed and acknowledged by the said George Bernard Shaw the Testator as and for his last Will and Testament in the presence of us who in his presence at his request and in the presence of each other all being present at the same time have hereunto subscribed our names as witnesses

G. Bernard Shaw

E. Marjorie White Married woman
    22 Compton Avenue, Luton, Beds.
Harold O. White, Master Printer,
    22 Compton Avenue, Luton, Beds.

APPENDIX C

NATIONAL GALLERY OF IRELAND
PRINCIPAL PURCHASES FROM THE SHAW FUND

(Artists' first names are only given to distinguish between common surnames, or to detail relatively minor artists. Figures in left column are catalogue numbers. Date purchased is given in brackets.)

Paintings, watercolours and drawings

1384 Domenico Tintoretto, *Venice, Queen of the Adriatic*, (1959)
1385 Domenico Ghirlandaio, *(?) Portrait of Clarice Orsini*, (1959)
1645 Louis Le Nain, *Adoration of the Shepherds*, (1961)
1646 Jean Nattier, *Carlotta Frederika Sparre, Countess Fersen*, (1961)
3315 Maurice Quentin De La Tour, *Louis Auguste Thibault-Dunois*, (1961)
1719 Murillo, *The Holy Family*, (1962)
1720 Murillo, *St Mary Magdalen*, (1962)
1721 El Mudo, *Abraham welcoming the three angels*, (1962)
1722 Courbet, *Dr Adolphe Marlet*, (1962)
1723 Boucher, *A young girl in a park*, (1962)
1737 Jack B. Yeats, *The double jockey act*, (1963)
1766 Jack B. Yeats, *About to write a letter*, (1964)
1768 Giovanni Di Paolo, *Crucifix*, (1964)
1769 Jack B. Yeats, *Grief*, (1965)
1760 Jacques Iverny, *The Annunciation*, (1965)
1790 Nathaniel Hone, The Elder, *The Conjurer*, (1966)
1812 Cigoli, *The Siege*, (1967)
1822 Marquet, *Porquerolles*, (1967)
1824 Roslin, *Le Marquis de Vaudreuil*, (1967)
1835–58 Various Schools, *Twenty-four icons* (The Allen Collection), (1968)
1867 La Tour, *The Image of Saint Alexis*, (1968)
1859 Walter Osborne, *Portrait of a gentleman*, (1968)
1860 Thomas Hickey, *Colonel William Kirkpatrick*, (1968)
1928 Goya, *El Sueño*, (1969)
4025 Valencian School, *Landscape with canopy and a legionary*, (1971)
4026 Valencian School, *Landscape with an angel bearing a martyr's crown*, (1971)
1982 Vouet, *The four seasons*, (1971)
4050 Eva Gonzales, *Two children playing on sand dunes*, (1972)

4052   Thomas Roberts, *A landscape*, (1972)

7515–33   Francis Place, *Twenty-three drawings*, (1972)

4055   Baron Gérard, *Marie-Julie Bonaparte, Queen of Spain, with her daughters, Zenaïde and Charlotte*, (1972)

4060   Jacques-Louis David, *The funeral of Patroclus*, (1973)

4074   Nathaniel Grogan, *A view towards Cork, on the river Lee*, (1973)

4089   Sogliani, *The Virgin and Child with St John the Baptist*, (1974)

4137   William Ashford, *A view of Dublin from Marino*, (1976)

4138   William Ashford, *A view of Dublin from Chapelizod*, (1976)

4170   French School, *Large apse*, (1976)

4171   French School, *Small apse*, (1976)

4186   Juan Fernandez, *A still life with citrons, a knife etc*, (1976)

4303   Nathaniel Grogan, *A harbour in County Cork*, (1978)

4304   Philip Hussey, *An interior with members of a family*, (1978)

4313   Fragonard, *Venus and Cupid*, (1978)

4315   Provoost, *Triptych: Virgin and Child with saints*, (1979)

4326   Reynolds, *The Right Honourable John Hely-Hutchinson*, (1979)

4339   Wheatley, *The Marquess and Marchioness of Antrim*, (1980)

4355   Van Dongen, *Stella in a flowered hat*, (1981)

4361   Signac, *Lady on a terrace, Saint-Tropez*, (1982)

4367   Henry Brooke, *The continence of Scipio*, (1982)

4468   Italian School, *A young man of the Branconio family (c. 1610)*, (1983)

4459   Camille Pissarro, *A bouquet of flowers in a vase*, (1983)

4463–66   Thomas Roberts, *Lucan House and three views in the demesne*, (1983)

4485   Soutine, *Man walking the stairs*, (1984)

4490   Nolde, *Two women in a garden*, (1984)

4508   William Ashford, *A bowl of flowers*, (1985)

Sculptures

8011   Renoir, *Pendule: hymne à la vie*, (1966)

8030   Duquesnoy, *Cardinal Guido Bentivoglio*, (1967)

8031   Attr. Juan Alonso Villabrille y Ron, *Elias overthrowing the false prophets of Baal*, (1967)

8028/29   Attr. Brustolon, *A pair of jardinières*, (1967)

8049   Ghiberti workshop, *Virgin and Child*, (1968)

8050   Courbet, *Madame Buchon*, (1968)

8051   Attr. Caffieri, *Bust of a lady*, (1968)

8052   Thomas Kirk, *Judge Charles Burton*, (1968)

8081   Dietz, *Chronos eating one of his children*, (1970)

8246   Richier, *The Virgin*, (1978)

8247   Richier, *St John the Evangelist*, (1978)

8303   Lawrence MacDonald, *Eurydice*, (1984)

APPENDIX D

FILMS MADE FROM SHAW'S PLAYS
*(Original Shaw titles are given in square brackets
below the film title, where they differ)*

Roman Boxera (Czechoslovakia)

[*Cashel Byron's Profession*]

FIRST SHOWING	1921
DIRECTOR	Vaclav Binovec
PRODUCER	Weteb Studios
SCREENPLAY	Suzanne Marwille
CAST INCLUDES	Frank: Frank Rose-Ruzicka
	Marta: Suzanne Marwille
	Theodor: V. Ch. Vladimirov

Cathedral Scene from Saint Joan (UK)

FIRST SHOWING	July/August 1927 (London)
DIRECTOR	Widgey Newman
PRODUCER	Vivian Van Dam (for the DeForest Phonofilm Company)
SCREENPLAY	Bernard Shaw
CAST INCLUDES	Saint Joan: Sybil Thorndike

How He Lied to Her Husband (UK)

FIRST SHOWING	12 January 1931 (London)
DIRECTOR	Cecil Lewis
PRODUCER	John Maxwell (for British International Pictures)
SCREENPLAY	Bernard Shaw
CAST INCLUDES	Herself: Vera Lennox
	Her Lover: Robert Harris
	Her Husband: Edmund Gwenn

Arms and the Man (UK)

FIRST SHOWINGS	4 August 1932 (Malvern Festival)
	24 September 1932 (London)
DIRECTOR	Cecil Lewis
PRODUCER	John Maxwell (for British International Pictures)
SCREENPLAY	Bernard Shaw
CAST INCLUDES	Paul Petkoff: Frederick Lloyd
	Bluntschli: Barry Jones
	Sergius Saranoff: Maurice Colbourne
	Raina: Anne Grey
	Catherine: Margaret Scudamore
	Louka: Angela Baddeley

Pygmalion (Germany)

FIRST SHOWING	2 September 1935 (Berlin)
DIRECTOR	Erich Engel
PRODUCER	Eberhard Klagemann (for Klagemann Film der Tobis-Rota)
SCREENPLAY	Heinrich Oberländer and Walter Wassermann
CAST INCLUDES	Eliza Doolittle: Jenny Jugo
	Henry Higgins: Gustaf Gründgens
	Col. Pickering: Anton Edthofer
	Alfred Doolittle: Eugen Klöpfer

Pygmalion (The Netherlands)

FIRST SHOWING	March 1937 (Amsterdam)
DIRECTOR	Ludwig Berger
PRODUCER	Rudolph Meyer (for Filmex Cinetone of Amsterdam)
SCREENPLAY	Ludwig Berger
CAST INCLUDES	Eliza Doolittle: Lily Bouwmeester
	Henry Higgins: Johan de Meester
	Col. Pickering: Eduard Verkade
	Alfred Doolittle: Matthieu van Eysden

Pygmalion (UK)

FIRST SHOWINGS	6 October 1938 (London)
	7 December 1938 (New York)

DIRECTORS	Anthony Asquith and Leslie Howard
PRODUCER	Gabriel Pascal
SCREENPLAY	Bernard Shaw (with additional dialogue by W.P. Lipscomb and Cecil Lewis)
MUSIC	Arthur Honegger
COSTUMES	Worth and Schiaparelli/Prof. Czettell
CAST INCLUDES	Eliza Doolittle: Wendy Hiller
	Henry Higgins: Leslie Howard
	Col. Pickering: Scott Sunderland
	Alfred Doolittle: Wilfrid Lawson
	Mrs Higgins: Marie Lohr

Major Barbara (UK)

FIRST SHOWINGS	7 April 1941 (London)
	13 May 1941 (New York)
DIRECTOR	Gabriel Pascal
PRODUCER	Gabriel Pascal
SCREENPLAY	Bernard Shaw
MUSIC	William Walton
COSTUMES	Cecil Beaton
CAST INCLUDES	Major Barbara: Wendy Hiller
	Adolphus Cusins: Rex Harrison
	Undershaft: Robert Morley
	Bill Walker: Robert Newton
	Snobby Price: Emlyn Williams
	The General: Sybil Thorndike
	Lady Britomart: Marie Lohr
	Jenny Hill: Deborah Kerr
	Policeman: Stanley Holloway
	James: Felix Aylmer

Caesar and Cleopatra (UK)

FIRST SHOWINGS	13 December 1945 (London)
	5 September 1946 (New York)
DIRECTOR	Gabriel Pascal
PRODUCER	Gabriel Pascal (for Rank Organisation)
SCREENPLAY	Bernard Shaw
MUSIC	Georges Auric
COSTUMES	Oliver Messel
CAST INCLUDES	Caesar: Claude Rains

Cleopatra: Vivien Leigh
Ftatateeta: Flora Robson
Pothinus: Francis L. Sullivan
Rufio: Basil Sydney
Britannus: Cecil Parker
Apollodorus: Stewart Granger
Belzanor: Stanley Holloway
Harp Girl: Jean Simmons
1st Nobleman: Felix Aylmer

Androcles and the Lion (USA)

FIRST SHOWINGS	14 January 1953 (New York)
	16 October 1953 (London)
DIRECTOR	Chester Erskine
PRODUCER	Gabriel Pascal (for RKO Pictures)
SCREENPLAY	Chester Erskine and Ken Englund
CAST INCLUDES	The Emperor: Maurice Evans
	The Captain: Victor Mature
	Androcles: Alan Young
	Lavinia: Jean Simmons
	Megaera: Elsa Lanchester
	Ferrovius: Robert Newton

Saint Joan (USA)

FIRST SHOWINGS	11 May 1957 (Paris)
	19 June 1957 (London)
	26 June 1957 (New York)
DIRECTOR	Otto Preminger
PRODUCER	Otto Preminger (for United Artists)
SCREENPLAY	Graham Greene
CAST INCLUDES	Saint Joan: Jean Seberg
	The Dauphin: Richard Widmark
	Dunois: Richard Todd
	Earl of Warwick: John Gielgud
	John de Stogumber: Harry Andrews
	De Courcelles: Barry Jones
	The Inquisitor: Felix Aylmer

The Doctor's Dilemma (UK)

FIRST SHOWINGS	17 December 1958 (New York)
	23 April 1959 (London)

DIRECTOR	Anthony Asquith
PRODUCER	Anatole de Grunwald (for Metro Goldwyn Mayer)
SCREENPLAY	Anatole de Grunwald
COSTUMES	Cecil Beaton
CAST INCLUDES	Jennifer Dubedat: Leslie Caron
	Louis Dubedat: Dirk Bogarde
	Sir Ralph Bloomfield Bonington: Robert Morley
	Cutler Walpole: Alastair Sim
	Sir Patrick Cullen: Felix Aylmer

Helden (Germany)

[Arms and the Man]

FIRST SHOWING	17 December 1958 (Hamburg)
DIRECTOR	Franz Peter Wirth
PRODUCERS	H. R. Sokal and P. Goldbaum (for Bavaria-Filmkunst)
SCREENPLAY	Johanna Sibelius and Eberhard Keindorff
CAST INCLUDES	Paul Petkoff: Kurt Kasznar
	Sergius Saranoff: Jan Hendricks
	Bluntschli: O. W. Fischer
	Nicola: Manfred Inger

Frau Warrens Gewerbe (Germany)

[Mrs Warren's Profession]

FIRST SHOWING	12 January 1960 (Hanover)
DIRECTOR	Akos von Rathony
PRODUCER	Heinz-Günter Sass (for Real Film GmbH)
SCREENPLAY	Johanna Sibelius and Eberhard Keindorff, from a screenplay by Anatole de Grunwald
CAST INCLUDES	Frau Warren: Lilli Palmer

The Devil's Disciple (USA)

FIRST SHOWINGS	20 August 1959 (New York)
	2 September 1959 (London)
DIRECTOR	Guy Hamilton
PRODUCER	Harold Hecht (for Brynaprod, SA, and Hecht-Hill-Lancaster Films Ltd)

SCREENPLAY   John Dighton and Roland Kibbee
CAST INCLUDES   Revd Anthony Anderson: Burt Lancaster
                    Dick Dudgeon: Kirk Douglas
                    General Burgoyne: Laurence Olivier
                    Judith Anderson: Janette Scott

The Millionairess (UK)

FIRST SHOWINGS   20 October 1960 (London)
                    9 February 1961 (New York)
DIRECTOR   Anthony Asquith
PRODUCER   Pierre Rouve (for Dimitri de Grunwald)
SCREENPLAY   Wolf Mankowitz
COSTUMES   Pierre Balmain
CAST INCLUDES   Epifania: Sophia Loren
                    Dr Kabir: Peter Sellers
                    Sagamore: Alastair Sim

My Fair Lady (USA)
[Musical based on *Pygmalion*]

FIRST SHOWING   October 1964 (New York)
DIRECTOR   George Cukor
PRODUCER   Jack L. Warner (for CBS/Warner)
SCREENPLAY   Alan J. Lerner
MUSIC   adapted by André Previn from the original score
                    by Frederick Loewe
COSTUMES   Cecil Beaton
CAST INCLUDES   Eliza Doolittle: Audrey Hepburn
                    Henry Higgins: Rex Harrison
                    Alfred Doolittle: Stanley Holloway
                    Col. Pickering: Wilfred Hyde-White
                    Mrs Higgins: Gladys Cooper

Great Catherine (UK)

FIRST SHOWING   1968 (London)
DIRECTOR   Gordon Flemyng
PRODUCER   Jules Buck (Warner/Keep Films)
SCREENPLAY   Hugh Leonard

CAST INCLUDES   Catherine the Great: Jeanne Moreau
Captain Edstaston: Peter O'Toole
Prince Patiomkin: Zero Mostel
The Sergeant: Akim Tamiroff
Sir George Gorse: Jack Hawkins

ACKNOWLEDGEMENTS

My valiant team has stayed with me to the end: Sarah Johnson (who made my words legible), Margery Morgan (who helped to make them more accurate), Richard Bates (who transferred the corrected text on to disc) and Vivian Elliot who has switched her attention from quotations to notations. I am sincerely grateful to them all.

Alison Samuel at Chatto & Windus has continued steering a hazardous course between house style and my own way of doing things. Joe Fox at Random House in the United States has kept a distant eye on everything.

I would like to renew my thanks to all those individuals and institutions mentioned in the previous three volumes (*The Search for Love*, *The Pursuit of Power* and *The Lure of Fantasy*), and in particular to Bernard Dukore, T. F. Evans, David and Susannah Marcus, Richard O'Donoghue, Barbara Smoker and Roma Woodnutt for their additional help with *The Last Laugh*. I also owe thanks to Sir Richard Attenborough, Sir Dirk Bogarde, K. Byrne, Karin Fernald, Mark Fisher, Philip French, Tom Geddes, Sir John Gielgud, Geoffrey C. Grant, Baroness Jeger, Helen Langdon, Mark Le Fanu, Hugh Leonard, Nora Lever, Donal McGahon, Aidan J. McGovern, Wolf Mankowitz, Michael Martin, Christopher Newton, Anthea Palmer, His Honour Judge David Pitman, Michael Purcell, Norman Sherry, Norman Wisdom, Michael Wynne.

I have also received assistance from a number of organizations: Academy of Motion Picture Arts and Sciences (California), Anglo–Swedish Literary Foundation, British Film Institute, Forás Éireann, International Shaw Summer School (Dublin), National Trust, Shaw Birthplace Museum Trust (Dublin), Shaw Festival Committee at Carlow, Shaw Society (Britain), Cultural Section of the Embassy of Sweden (London), Swedish English Literary Translators' Association, Trust and Custodial Services Bank of Ireland (Dublin).

INDEX

Actors' Orphanage, 40, 104
Adams, Elbridge, 88
Admirable Bashville, The, see Shaw:
    Works
Albert, Sidney P., 88
Allan, Andrew, 75
alphabetical reform, 3, 6, 10–21
    passim, 22, 25; competition 21–3;
    see also Androcles and the Lion
    (transliteration) *under* Shaw:
    Works
American Repertory Theatre, 90
American Theater Council, 20
American Women's Club, Dublin, 85
Anderson, Dr Robert, 89
Andersson, Ingvar, 39
Andrews, Harry, 64
Andrews, Julie, 9–10, 62
Androcles and the Lion, see Shaw:
    Works
Anglo-Swedish Literary Foundation,
    38–9
Annan, Lord (Noël), 27, 89
Antony and Cleopatra, 73
Apple Cart, The, see Shaw: *Works*
Arch Editeur, L', 72
Archer, William, 60, 88
Arms and the Man, see Shaw: *Works*
Ashford, William: *A bowl of flowers*,
    33, 118
Asquith, Anthony, 66, 67, 68, 69, 70
Astor, Lady (Nancy), 5, 45, 57, 88
Astor, Viscount (William Waldorf), 89
Atkins, Eileen, 73
Attenborough, Sir Richard, 30
Attlee, Clement, 4, 5
Aylmer, Sir Felix, 29, 64, 67
Ayot St Lawrence, 41–2; *see also*
    'Shaw's Corner'

Back to Methuselah, see Shaw: *Works*
Balcon, Sir Michael, 29
Bank of Ireland, 9
Barber, Elizabeth, 80
Barber, Frances, 90
Barrie, J. M.: estate, 3
Bassett, Eric, 52–3, 57, 58
Baulkwill, Sir Reginald (Public
    Trustee), 20–1, 22, 23, 24

Beaton, Cecil, 10, 63, 66
Beech, Patrick, 103
Beech, Stella (*née* Campbell), 103
Beerbohm, Max, 60
Bentley, Eric, 60, 79
Bergman, Hjalmar, 38
Bergman, Ingrid, 73
Bevan, E. Dean: *A Concordance of the
    plays and prefaces of Bernard
    Shaw*, 59
Billington, Michael, 77, 87
Bilton, Alice, 92, 107
Bilton, Margaret, 92, 106–7
biographies, Shaw, 40, 53, 61–2,
    79–83
Birk, Baroness (Alma), 89
Birkett, Lord, 18
Birmingham Post, 47
Black Girl, The, see Shaw: *Works*
Bodley Head, The 18; *The Bodley
    Head Bernard Shaw Collected
    Plays and their Prefaces*, 58
Bogarde, Sir Dirk, 66, 67
Böll, Heinrich and Marie, 72
Borges, Jorge Luis, 78
Boyle, Sir Edward (Baron Boyle of
    Handsworth), 26, 27, 30–1, 89
Brecht, Bertold, 78; *A Respectable
    Wedding*, 76
Bridge, Peter, 74
Brien, Alan, 79
Briers, Richard, 29, 72
British Library: separates from British
    Museum, 27; donations received
    from British Museum, 27–8,
    88–9; British Library Act 1972,
    89; *see also* British Museum
British Museum: challenges validity of
    alphabet trusts, 11, 13, 15, 20–1 ;
    income received from Shaw
    estate, 26–7, 31, 88, 89; Shaw's
    intentions towards, 30, 31–2,
    89–90, 112; Manuscript
    Department, 31, 32 87; *see also*
    British Library
Brophy, Brigid, 54, 61
Brown, Ivor, 41, 47
Buoyant Billions, see Shaw: *Works*
Burgess, Anthony, ix

Burton, Robert, 64
Butler, R. A., 5
Butler, Samuel: *Erewhon*, 3

Caesar and Cleopatra, see Shaw: *Works*
Callow, Simon, 72
Campbell, Lady Colin, 87
Campbell, Mrs Patrick, 103
Canadian Broadcasting Corp., 75
Candida, see Shaw: *Works*
Captain Brassbound's Conversion, see
    Shaw: *Works*
Carlow, Ireland: Shaw's property in,
    35–8; Shaw Festival (1991), 38
Carlow Nationalist, 35
Caron, Leslie, 66–7
Casserley, C. J., 49
Casson, Sir Lewis, 5
Castelli, Cesare, 72
Catholic Action, 65
Cavendish, Nicola, 76
Chaplin, Charlie, 54
Chesterton, G. K.: Shaw to, 79;
    estate, 3
Chocolate Soldier, The, 56
Cigoli: *The Siege*, 34, 117
Clunes, Alec, 74
Cockerell, Sydney, 57, 71–2
Colbourne, Maurice, 75
Colthurst, Cecily, 7, 95
Combe, Shournagh Dorothy, 95
Conrad, Joseph, 60
Constable & Co., 18, 114
Conti, Tom, 74
Costello, Donald P., 67
Coward, Noël, 71
Cox, Brian, 87
Craig, Edy: Shaw to, 31
Cuckor, George, 63

Daily Mail, 23
Daily Telegraph, The, 20
Dankworth, Johnny, 71
David, Jacques-Louis: *The funeral of*
    Patroclus, 34, 118
Davies, Brian (Public Trustee), 26
Day, Frances, 54
Day, Frederick, 11, 92, 107
Day Margaret, 107
Dench, Judi, 72
Devil's Disciple, The, see Shaw: *Works*
Dexter, John, 74
Doctor's Dilemma, The, see Shaw:
    Works
Dodson, Alan, 21
Doherty, Brian, 75–6

Don Juan in Hell, see Shaw: *Works*
Dors, Diana, 11
Douglas, Kirk, 67, 68, 69
Dublin: Holroyd's Shavian research
    in, 80–1; Municipal Gallery, 8,
    48, 103; National Library, 48;
    Shaw's birthplace (33 Synge
    Street), 32–3, 40, 85–6; Shaw
    Summer School, 85, *see also*
    National Gallery of Ireland,
    commemorative tree-planting,
    86*n*; Dublin Tourism, 86*n*
Dukore, Bernard F.: *The Collected*
    Screenplays of Bernard Shaw, 59
Dunlop, Frank, 74
Duquesnoy, François: *Cardinal Guido*
    Bentivoglio, 34–5, 118

Eccles, Viscount (David), 89
Economist, The, 3
Edel, Leon, 58
Edwards, Christopher, 87
Elgar, Edward: Shaw to, 26
Eliot, T. S., 53, 63; (quoted), 5, 48
Elphinstone, K. E., 13
Ervine, St John, 5; *Bernard Shaw:*
    His Life, Work and Friends, 40,
    61, 80
Evans, Dame Edith, 41
Evans, Maurice, 55
Evans, T. F., 52, 76; *Shaw: The*
    Critical Heritage, 59
Evening News, 41
Evening Press, 86
Evening Standard, 47, 67, 70
Evershed, Lord (Raymond) 21
Everbody's Political What's What? see
    Shaw: *Works*
Eyre, Ronald, 74

Fabian Society, London, 105
Farfetched Fables, see Shaw: *Works*
Farleigh, John, 88
Fernald, John, 28–9
Fernald, Karin, 29
Festival of Britain (1951), 3–4, 5
Fields, Gracie, 54
film productions, 52, 54–5, 62–71, 90,
    119–25
Fisher, Mark, MP, 27, 89
Fitzmaurice, Major, 36, 37
Fitzwilliam Museum, Cambridge, 48,
    103–4
Flemyng, Gordon, 70
Forás Éireann, 9
Forster, E. M., 53, 63

Foundation for Sport and Arts, 30
Fountain Press, 88
Fox, Edward, 90
French, Philip, 71

Geddes, Tom, 39
Geijer, Erik Gustaf, 39
Geneva, see Shaw: *Works*
Gérard, Baron: *Marie-Julie Bonaparte*, 34, 118
Getting Married, see Shaw: *Works*
Gibbs, A. M.: *Shaw: Interviews and Recollections*, 59
Gielgud, Sir John, 64, 73
Giovanni di Paolo: *Crucifix*, 32, 117
Gold, Jack, 74
Goya, Francisco; *El Sueño*, 34, 117
Great Catherine, see Shaw: *Works*
Green, Benny, 61, 71
Greenaway, Peter, 71
Greene, Graham, 53, 63, 64, 65–6
Gregory, Lady Augusta, 88
Griffith, Kenneth, 70
Grogan, Nathaniel: landscapes 35, 118
Gross, John, 87
Grunwald, Anatole de, 66, 67
Guardian, 68, 77, 87
Gurly, Walter John, 35

Hagberg, Knut, 39
Haigh, Kenneth, 64
Hamilton, Guy, 68
Hamilton, Mary Penelope, 95
Hammond, Kay, 73
Hamon, Augustin, 72, 88
Hamon, Henriette, 72
Hankinson, Mary, 41
Hardman, David, MP, 45–6
Hardy, Thomas: estate, 3
Harman, Mr Justice, 11–12, 13, 14–15, 16, 17–18
Harrison, Rex, 19, 55, 63
Hart, Moss, 9
Hattersley, Roy, MP, 85
Haughey, Charles, 85, 86
Hauser, Frank, 73
Hawkins, Jack, 70
Hayward, Pascoe, KC, 7–8
Heaney, Seamus, 85
Heartbreak House, see Shaw: *Works*
Hecht, Harold, 67, 68
Henderson, Archibald, 6, 45, 57; *George Bernard Shaw: Man of the Century*, 61
Hepburn, Audrey, 62
Her First Roman, 71

Higgs, Clara, 92, 100
Higgs, Harry Batchelor, 92, 106, 107
Hildesheimer, Wolfgang, 72
Hirst, Sir Wyndham (Public Trustee), 10–11
Hodgman, Emma, 92, 106, 107
Hodgman, Kate, 92
Holland, Sir Edward Milner, QC, 13, 15–16
Holloway, Stanley, 9, 63
Hone, Nathaniel, the Elder: *The Conjurer*, 35, 117
House of Commons: debates on Shaw, 11, 19, 26, 27–8, 31, 32, 53, 89
Houston, Penelope, 65
How He Lied to Her Husband, see Shaw: *Works*
Howard, Alan, 90
Howard, Cornelius, 85
Hughes, Emrys, MP, 26, 32
Hughes, Howard, 54, 44
Hurry, Colin: 'Concerning the Dead', 2

Irish Independent, 9
Irish Press, 86
Irish Sailors' and Soldiers' Land Fund, 86
Irving, Laurence: Shaw to, 82
Isherwood, Christopher: *The Black Girl*, 71
Iverny, Jacques: *The Annunciation*, 34, 117

Jackson, Barry, 57
James, Henry, 58, 60
Jeger, Lena (Baroness Jeger of St Pancras), 53
Jenkins of Putney, Lord (Hugh), 89
Jitta's Atonement, see Shaw: *Works*
John, Augustus: painting, 43, 103
John Bull's Other Island, see Shaw: *Works*
Johnson, Eyvind, 38
Jones, Barry, 75
Jones, Professor Daniel, 15
Jones, Richard, 79
Joyce, James, 60

Keaveney, Raymond, 33
Keith Penelope, 72
King, Denis, 71
Kingsmill, Hugh, 83
Kipling Rudyard, 60

Labiche, Eugène, 3

Laden, Alice, 44, 46, 47, 50; *The George Bernard Shaw Vegetarian Cook Book*, 47
Lagerkvist, Pär, 38
Lancaster, Burt, 67, 68–9
Lane, Sir Allen, 24, 53
Langner, Lawrence, 57; Shaw to, 82
La Tour, Étienne: *The Image of Saint Alexis*, 34, 117
Laughton, Charles, 73
Laurence, Dan H., 40, 58–9; *Bernard Shaw: Collected Letters*, 88
Lawrence, D. H., 60
Lawrence, T. E., Charlotte Shaw's correspondence with, 88
Layton, Robert, 39
Lazarus, Robert, 13
Lee, Jennie (Baroness Lee of Asheridge) 27
Lee Vandeleur, 59, 62
Lees-Milne, James, 43, 46
Léhar, Franz, 56
Leigh, Vivien, 73
Lejeune, C. A., 70
Le Nain, Louis: *Adoration of the Shepherds*, 34, 117
Leon, Jack and Beatrice, 74
Leonard, Hugh, 70
Lerner, Alan J., 9
Lever, Nora, 85–6
Levey, Sir Michael, 33
Levy, Benn, 46
Lindgren, Torgny, 39
Littlewood, Joan, 75
Loewe, Frederick, 9
Loewenstein, Dr Fritz, 42–3, 44–6, 47, 49, 50–2, 57–8, 114, *Bernard Shaw through the Camera*, 58
Lohr, Marie, 70
London School of Economics, 48
London theatres: Albery, 74; Aldwych, 74; Arts, 74; Everyman, Hampstead, 74; Globe, 72; Greenwich, 90; Hampstead, 78, 86, 87–8; Lyric, Hammersmith, 74; Mermaid, 72, 74, 78; National, 48, 72, 75, 78, 90; Old Vic, 72, 74; 'Q', 74; Royal Court, 73, 75
Loren, Sophia, 69, 70
Love Among the Artists, see Shaw: *Works*
Lyth, Jisbella, 41

MacCarthy, Sir Desmond, 60
MacCarthy, Peter, 21, 23, 24, 25–6

McCowen, Alec, 74, 90
Macdona Players, 73
McKellen, Ian, 72, 74
Mackendrick, Alexander, 68
McLachlan, Dame Laurentia: Shaw to, 77
Macmillan, Harold (Lord Stockton), 11
Magrath, J. F., 23
Major Barbara, see Shaw: *Works*
Man and Superman, see Shaw: *Works*
Manchester Guardian, 5, 8, 11–12, 14, 47
Mankowitz, Wolf, 69
Manningham-Buller, Sir Reginald, (Attorney General), 13, 19, 20, 53
Mappin & Webb, 22
Marshall, Christabell, 88
Martinson, Harry, 38
Marx, Harpo, 55
Mature, Victor, 55
Meisel, Martin: *Shaw and the Nineteenth Century Theater*, 60
Meredith, Georgina, 107
Metro-Goldwyn-Mayer (MGM), 56, 66
Metropolitan Museum, New York, 48
Miles, Bernard, 74
Millionairess, The, see Shaw: *Works*
Misalliance, see Shaw: *Works*
Mrs Warren's Profession, see Shaw: *Works*
Molnar, Ferenc, 56
Mondadori, Arnoldo, 72
Morahan, Christopher, 78
Moreau, Jeanne, 70
Morgan, Margery, 60, 78
Morley, Robert, 67
Morley, Sheridan, 79
Morse, Barry, 75
Mostel, Zero, 70
Muir, Kenneth, 60
Municipal Gallery, Dublin, 48
Murillo, Bartolomé: *The Holy Family*, 32, 34, 117; *St Mary Magdalen*, 32, 34, 117
Murray, Gilbert, 88
Murray, Stephen, 72
Musters, Georgina, 107
My Dear Dorothea, see Shaw: *Works*
My Fair Lady, ix, 9–10, 22, 52, 55, 62–3, 90, 124

National City Bank Ltd, Dublin, 7, 8, 9, 91

National Gallery of Ireland, 8, 13, 80, 86, 112, purchases from Shaw Fund, 32, 33–5, 117–18
National Library, Dublin, 48
National Portrait Gallery, London, 48, 90, 104
National Provincial Bank Ltd, 6, 91
National Trust, the: and 'Shaw's Corner' 4, 41, 42, 43–4, 46, 47, 49–50, 104, negotiations with Loewenstein, 42–3, 44–6, 49; and Shaw Memorial Fund Appeal, 5, 46, 47–8; auctions Shaw's possessions, 48; Shaw to, 43, 44
New Statesman, 65, 73, 88
New York Times, 54, 55
News Chronicle, 8
News of the World, 41
Hewton, Christopher, 76, 77
Newton, Robert, 55
Niagara-on-the-Lake, Ontario: Shaw Festival, 59, 75–7
Nicolson, Sir Harold, 45, 46
Nobel Prize for Literature, Shaw's, 38
Nunn, Trevor, 90

O'Bolger, Demetrius, 62
Observer, The, 1, 70
O'Casey, Sean, 41, 57
Official Trustee Act (1906), 10
O'Flaherty V.C., see Shaw: *Works*
Olivier, Lord (Laurence), 69, 72–3
On the Rocks, see Shaw: *Works*
Ormerod, Lord Justice, 21
Osborne, John: *Look Back in Anger*, 73
O'Toole, Peter, 29, 70, 73
Oxford History of English Literature, The, 60

Pall Mall Gazette, 88
Palmer, Lilli, 67
Parker, John, MP, 27
Parliament, *see* House of Commons debates
Pascal, Gabriel, 41, 45, 54–5, 56, 57, 68, 88
Pascal, Valerie, 55, 56
Passion Play, see Shaw:*Works*
Patch, Blanche, 44, 46, 49, 57, 100, 114; *Thirty Years with G.B.S.*, 53
Patterson, Jenny, 87
Pearson, Hesketh, 57; *Bernard Shaw: His Life and Personality*, 61; *G.B.S., A. Postscript*, 53

Penguin Books, 24, 86n
Percy, Esmé, 73; Shaw to, 40
Philanderer, The, see Shaw: Works
Phonetic Alphabet Association, 13, 14
Pimlott, Steven, 79
Pitman, Sir Isaac: *Introduction to Phonography*, 22
Pitman, Sir James, 15, 18–20, 21–2, 23, 24–5, 26, 30, 32; Shaw to, 12, 18, 22
Plays Unpleasant, see Shaw: Works
Power, Tyrone, 73
Preminger, Otto, 63–5
Previn, André, 63
Pritt, D. N., 45
Pryde, Bill, 74
Public Trustee, the, 10, 11, 52–3
'Public Trustee v. Day and others', 11–16; judgement, 16, 17–18; appeal, 20–1
Pugmire, Dr S. L., 23
Pygmalion, see Shaw: Works

Quaritch (Bernard) Ltd., 88

RADA, *see* Royal Academy of Dramatic Art
Rathbone, Jack, 44, 45, 46, 49
Rathony, Akos von, 67
Rattigan, Terence, 67, 68
Read, Kingsley, 23, 24
Redgrave, Vanessa, 90
Renfrew of Kaimsthorn, Lord (Andrew), 89
Renton, Tim, MP, 27–8
Richard, Cliff, 69
Richardson, Sir Ralph, 73
Richier, Ligier: *St John the Evangelist*, 34, 118, *The Virgin*, 34, 118
Richter, Mrs Clara, 20
Rigg, Diana, 74
RKO Studios, 54, 55
Robinson, Mary, 85
Rodin, Auguste: bust, 43, 103
Rogers, Eames Bagenal, 107
Romer, Lord Justice, 21
Roslin, Alexandre: *Le Marquis de Vaudreuil*, 34, 117
Rosset, B. C.: *Shaw of Dublin: The Formative Years*, 62
Rouve, Pierre, 69
Royal Academy of Dramatic Art (RADA), 13–14, 15, 28–31, 80, 112
Royal Shakespeare Company, 74
Royal Society of Literature, 5

Russell, Sir Charles, KC (QC), 7, 13, 14–15, 16

Saint Joan, see, Shaw: Works
'St John, Christopher', see Marshall, Christabell
Sargent, John Singer: drawing of Harley Granville-Barker, 108
Schlesinger, John, 72
Schmoller, Hans, 24
Schneider, Eva Maria, 107
Scofield, Paul, 64, 90
Scotsman, The, 25
Scott, Janette, 68
Seberg, Jean, 63, 64
Sellers, Peter, 69
Shakes versus Shav, see Shaw: Works
Shakespeare, William: Cymbeline, 77; Hamlet, 78; Othello, 79
Shakespeare Memorial National Theatre, 40, 103
Shavian, The, 20, 52, 57, 66, 76
Shaw, Charlotte, 44; correspondence with T. E. Lawrence, 88; will, 6–9, 91–104
Shaw, George Bernard:
  Estate: gross value, 3; net value, 6, 11; death duties on, 6, 11, 30; Will, 3, 6, 10–11, 16–17, 50–1, 52–3, 59, 111–15; annuities, 6, 105–9; see also British Museum, National Gallery of Ireland, Royal Academy of Dramatic Art; High Court case over, see 'Public Trustee v. Day and Others'
  academic assessments, 60–1
  biographies, 40, 53, 61–2, 79–83
  copyright royalties, 3, 4, 6, 10, 13, 27
  films, 52, 54–5, 62–71, 90, 119–25
  musicals, 71, see also My Fair Lady
  posthumous publications, 54, 58–9, 71, 88
  revival of plays, 72–8, 86–8, 90
  Shaw's letters to:
  Edy Craig, on the British Museum, 31
  Major Fitzmaurice, on the Carlow properties, 36, 37; on Socialism, 37
  Laurence Irving, on writing a biography of his father, 82
  Lawrence Langner, on himself, 82
  National Trust, on 'Shaw's Corner', 43; on the Shaw Societies, 43; on the Winstens, 44

James Pitman, on his alfabet trusts, 12, 18, 22
Ellen Terry, on the Carlow properties, 35
Shaw's views on:
  adapting his plays, 77
  alphabetical reform, 12, 16–17, 18, 22, 110–12
  appeals for money, 39–40
  biographies, 82
  British Museum, 31
  his Carlow properties, 35, 36, 37
  communism, 61
  his dramatic methods, 79
  history, 61
  money, ix, 12, 46, 48, 85
  musical versions of his plays, 56–7
  Public Trustees, 10, 52–3
  his being a realist, 78, 79
  schoolbooks of his works, 59
  Shaw Societies, 43
  Works:
  The Admirable Bashville (muscial), 71
  Androcles and the Lion, 16, 82,; films, 54–5, 122; musical, 71; phonetic transliteration, 12, 23–5
  The Apple Cart, 73, 85
  Arms and the Man, 56, 72; film 67, 120, 123
  Back to Methuselah, 74
  The Black Girl, 71
  Buoyant Billions, Farfetched Fables, & Shakes versus Shav, 54
  Caesar and Cleopatra, 70, 71, 73, 90; film, 121
  Candida (film), 54
  Captain Brassbound's Comversion, 56, 72, 73
  Cashel Byron's Profession; film, 119
  The Devil's Disciple, 71, 73, 74; film, 67–9,
  The Doctor's Dilemma, 72, 87; film 66–7, 123–4
  Don Juan in Hell, 75, 76
  Everybody's Political What's What?, 36, 85
  Geneva, 78, 85
    Getting Married, 76, 87
  Great Catherine (film), 70, 124–5
  Heartbreak House, 63, 72, 74, 76, 87, 89
  How He Lied to Her Husband, 38; film, 119
  Jitta's Atonement, 57
  John Bull's Other Island, 81

Love Among the Artists, 71

Major Barbara, ix, 70, 71, 72, 73; film, 121

Man and Superman, 71, 72, 73, 76, 87, 89; film, 54

The Millionairess, 76; film, 69–70, 124

Misalliance, 76, 79, 87, 90

Mrs Warren's Profession, 2, 74, 87; films, 67, 90, 123

My Dear Dorothea, 59

O'Flaherty V.C., 74

On the Rocks, 72, 76

Passion Play, 59

The Philanderer, 78, 86–8

Plays Unpleasant, 78, 87

Pygmalion, 17, 52, 53, 56–7, 73, 74, 90; films, 120–1; *see also My Fair Lady*

Saint Joan, 59, 65, 73, 76; films, 63–6, 90, 119, 122

The Shewing-up of Blanco Posnet (film) 70

The Simpleton of the Unexpected Isles, 61, 76

Too True to be Good, 72, 74, 79

An Unsocial Socialist, 58

Valentine's Day, 90

Village Wooing, 72

Widowers' Houses, 74, 87

You Never Can Tell, 73, 76; musical, 71

Shaw, Lucinda Elizabeth, 62

Shaw Birthplace Trust, 32–3, 85–6 and *n*

Shaw Festivals: Carlow, 38; Niagara-on-the-Lake, 59, 75–7

Shaw Fund, 89

Shaw Memorial Fund Appeal (1951) 4, 5, 6, 46, 47

Shaw Review, The, 59, 70

Shaw's Corner, Ayot St Lawrence: the National Trust and, 4, 41, 42–6, 47–50, 104; opening of, 41, 46–7; play performances at, 52

Shaw Society, the, 14, 19, 20, 49, 51, 52–3, 58; Lowenstein and, 43, 44–5, 51, 52, 57; Presidents and Vice-presidents of, 27, 29, 57; *Bulletin*, 58; of Dublin, 86*n*

Shewing-up of Blanco Posnet, The, *see* Shaw: *Works*

Sight and Sound, 70

Sim, Alastair, 67

Simmons, Jean, 55

Simpleton of the Unexpected Isles, The,

see, see, Shaw: *Works*

Sinatra, Frank, 55

Smith, Mrs Ronald (*née* Margaret Cashin), 107

Smoker, Barbara, 13, 14, 15–16, 18–20, 21–2, 23, 24, 25, 26, 32, 52, 57, 64

Sobienowski, Floryan: Shaw to, 31

Society of Authors, the, 58, 80; accepts Greene as scriptwriter to *Saint Joan*, 63, 64–6; uncommercial contract on *Doctor's Dilemma*, 66; and dialogue changes to *Devil's Disciple*, 68; agrees to filming of *Millionairess*, 69; and ban on *Pygmalion*, 52, 53; Academic Advisory Committee formed, 58, 77, licences issued by, 72

Sondheim, Stephen, 71

Soper, Donald (later Baron Soper), 14

Sopwith, Sir Charles, 24, 26

Spectator, The, 87

Spender, Stephen, 53

Star, the, 6

Stewart, J. I. M.: *Eight Modern Writers*, 60

Stopes, Marie, 5

Strachey, Lytton, 82

Straus, Oscar, 56

Strobl, Sigmund de (also Sigismund): bust of Shaw, 103

Suhrkamp Verlag, 72

Sunday Graphic, 54

Sunday Press, 32, 86

Sunday Telegraph, 87

Sunday Times, 27, 28, 32

Swedish literature, *see* Anglo-Swedish Literary Foundation

Tamiroff, Akim, 70

Tate Gallery, the, 48, 104

Terry, Ellen, Shaw's correspondence with, 54, 88, 89; Shaw to, 35, 77, 81

theatre productions: London *see* London theatres; provincial, 73–4; *see also* Shaw Festivals

Thom, Ron, 76

Time and Tide, 41

Times, The, 11, 20, 23, 25, 53, 64, 69, 73, 74, 80, 89

Times Educational Supplement, 87

Todd, Susan, 73

Too True to be Good, *see* Shaw: *Works*

Topham, Sybil, 28

Treasury Department, the, 26, 30–1
Trebitsch, Siegfried, 45, 56, 57, 72
Trotter, David, 87
Troubetskoy, Paul: bust, 104
Trustees Act (1893), 9
Tyson, Brian (ed.): *Shaw's Book Reviews*, 88

United States; Shavian studies in, 58, 59, 60; centennial conference, 90
Unsocial Socialist, An, see Shaw: *Works*

Vaisey, Sir Harry, 6, 7, 8
Valentine's Day, 71
Valera, Éamon de, 37
Village Wooing, see Shaw: *Works*
Vouet: *The Four Seasons*, 34, 117

Walker, Alexander, 70
Walser, Martin, 72
Walsh, Gordon, 25
Walters, Ethel Gordon, 107
Wardle, Irving, 74
Warner Brothers, 62
Webb, Sidney (Lord Passfield), 7, 92
Weintraub, Stanley 58; *The Diaries*, 59; *Shaw: An Autobiography*, 59
Weldon, Fay, 90

Wells, H. G., 88; estate, 3
West, Rebecca, 4
Wheeler, Margaret, 88
Whelen, John Frederick Leman, 92
Whitehead, Paxton, 76
Whittaker, Herbert, 77
Widmark, Richard, 64
Widowers' Houses, see Shaw: *Works*
Wilde, Oscar: *The Soul of Man Under Socialism*, 81
Williams, Clifford, 72
Williams, Raymond: *Drama from Ibsen to Brecht*, 60; *Drama from Ibsen to Eliot*, 60
Wilson, Colin, 61
Wilson, Sir David, 27, 28
Winsten, Clare, 44, 46, 49
Winsten, Stephen, 44, 46
Wirth, Franz Peter, 67
Wisdom, Norman, 71
Wood, John, 74
Woolf, Leonard, 79
Wynne, Dr Michael, 33

Yeats, Jack: paintings, 35, 117
Yeats, W. B., 60
You Never Can Tell, see Shaw: *Works*
Young, Alan, 55

Discover more about our forthcoming books through Penguin's FREE newspaper...

Penguin Quarterly

It's packed with:

- exciting features
- author interviews
- previews & reviews
- books from your favourite films & TV series
- exclusive competitions & much, much more...

Write off for your free copy today to:
Dept JC
Penguin Books Ltd
FREEPOST
West Drayton
Middlesex
UB7 0BR
NO STAMP REQUIRED

READ MORE IN PENGUIN

In every corner of the world, on every subject under the sun, Penguin represents quality and variety – the very best in publishing today.

For complete information about books available from Penguin – including Puffins, Penguin Classics and Arkana – and how to order them, write to us at the appropriate address below. Please note that for copyright reasons the selection of books varies from country to country.

In the United Kingdom: Please write to *Dept. JC, Penguin Books Ltd, FREEPOST, West Drayton, Middlesex UB7 0BR*

If you have any difficulty in obtaining a title, please send your order with the correct money, plus ten per cent for postage and packaging, to *PO Box No. 11, West Drayton, Middlesex UB7 0BR*

In the United States: Please write to *Penguin USA Inc., 375 Hudson Street, New York, NY 10014*

In Canada: Please write to *Penguin Books Canada Ltd, 10 Alcorn Avenue, Suite 300, Tororto, Ontario M4V 3B2*

In Australia: Please write to *Penguin Books Australia Ltd, 487 Maroondah Highway, Ringwood, Victoria 3134*

In New Zealand: Please write to *Penguin Books (NZ) Ltd, 182–190 Wairau Road, Private Bag, Takapuna, Auckland 9*

In India: Please write to *Penguin Books India Pvt Ltd, 706 Eros Apartments, 56 Nehru Place, New Delhi 110 019*

In the Netherlands: Please write to *Penguin Books Netherlands B.V., Keizersgracht 231 NL–1016 DV Amsterdam*

In Germany: Please write to *Penguin Books Deutschland GmbH, Friedrichstrasse 10–12, W–6000 Frankfurt/Main 1*

In Spain: Please write to *Penguin Books S. A., C. San Bernardo 117–6° E–28015 Madrid*

In Italy: Please write to *Penguin Italia s.r.l., Via Felice Casati 20, I–20124 Milano*

In France: Please write to *Penguin France S. A., 17 rue Lejeune, F–31000 Toulouse*

In Japan: Please write to *Penguin Books Japan, Ishikiribashi Building, 2–5–4, Suido, Tokyo 112*

In Greece: Please write to *Penguin Hellas Ltd, Dimocritou 3, GR–106 71 Athens*

In South Africa: Please write to *Longman Penguin Southern Africa (Pty) Ltd, Private Bag X08, Bertsham 2013*

LITERARY BIOGRAPHIES AND AUTOBIOGRAPHIES

Emily Brontë	Katherine Frank
Coleridge: Early Visions	Richard Holmes
Charles Dickens	Edgar Johnson
The Life of Graham Greene	Norman Sherry
Reflections	Graham Greene
A Sort of Life	Graham Greene
The Young Thomas Hardy	Robert Gittings
John Keats	Robert Gittings
Rudyard Kipling	Charles Carrington
Katherine Mansfield: A Secret Life	Claire Tomalin
Prick Up Your Ears: The Biography of Joe Orton	John Lahr
Bitter Fame: A Life of Sylvia Plath	Anne Stevenson
Sartre: Romantic Rationalist	Iris Murdoch
Bernard Shaw	Michael Holroyd
Shelley	Richard Holmes
The Autobiography of Alice B. Toklas	Gertrude Stein
Dylan Thomas	Paul Ferris
Tolstoy	Henry Troyat
Tolstoy	A. N. Wilson
The Life and Death of Mary Wollstonecraft	Claire Tomalin
Yeats: The Man and the Mask	Richard Ellmann

READ MORE IN PENGUIN

A CHOICE OF NON-FICTION

Riding the Iron Rooster Paul Theroux

Travels in old and new China with the author of *The Great Railway Bazaar*. 'Mr Theroux cannot write badly ... he is endlessly curious about places and people ... and in the course of a year there was almost no train in the whole vast Chinese rail network in which he did not travel' – Ludovic Kennedy

Ninety-two Days Evelyn Waugh

In this fascinating chronicle of a South American journey, Waugh describes the isolated cattle country of Guiana, sparsely populated by an odd collection of visionaries, rogues and ranchers, and records the nightmarish experiences travelling on foot, by horse and by boat through the jungle in Brazil.

The Life of Graham Greene Norman Sherry
Volume One 1904–1939

'Probably the best biography ever of a living author' – Philip French in the *Listener*. Graham Greene has always maintained a discreet distance from his reading public.This volume reconstructs his first thirty-five years to create one of the most revealing literary biographies of the decade.

The Day Gone By Richard Adams

In this enchanting memoir the bestselling author of *Watership Down* tells his life story from his idyllic 1920s childhood spent in Newbury, Berkshire, through public school, Oxford and service in World War Two to his return home and his courtship of the girl he was to marry.

A Turn in the South V. S. Naipaul

'A supremely interesting, even poetic glimpse of a part of America foreigners either neglect or patronize' – *Guardian*. 'An extraordinary panorama' – *Daily Telegraph*. 'A fine book by a fine man, and one to be read with great enjoyment: a book of style, sagacity and wit' – *Sunday Times*

READ MORE IN PENGUIN

A CHOICE OF NON-FICTION

Ginsberg: A Biography Barry Miles

The definitive life of one of this century's most colourful poets. 'A life so dramatic, so dangerous, so committed to hard-volume truth, that his survival is a miracle, his kindness, wisdom and modesty a blessing' – *The Times*. 'Read it to the end' – Michael Horovitz

Coleridge: Early Visions Richard Holmes

'Dazzling ... Holmes has not merely reinterpreted Coleridge; he has re-created him, and his biography has the aura of fiction, the shimmer of an authentic portrait ... a biography like few I have ever read' –*Guardian*. 'Coleridge lives, and talks and loves ... in these pages as never before' – *Independent*

The Speeches of Winston Churchill David Cannadine (ed.)

The most eloquent statesman of his time, Winston Churchill used language as his most powerful weapon. These orations, spanning fifty years, show him gradually honing his rhetoric until, with spectacular effect, 'he mobilized the English language, and sent it into battle'.

Higher than Hope Fatima Meer

A dramatic, personal and intimate biography drawing on letters and reminiscences from Nelson Mandela himself and his close family, *Higher Than Hope* is an important tribute to one of the greatest living figures of our time. It is also a perceptive commentary on the situation in South Africa. No one concerned with politics or humanity can afford to miss it.

Among the Russians Colin Thubron

'The Thubron approach to travelling has an integrity that belongs to another age. And this author's way with words gives his books a value far transcending their topical interest; it is safe to predict that they will be read a century hence' – Dervla Murphy in the *Irish Times*

READ MORE IN PENGUIN

A CHOICE OF NON-FICTION

Citizens A Chronicle of the French Revolution   Simon Schama

'The most marvellous book I have read about the French Revolution in the last fifty years' – Richard Cobb in *The Times*. 'He has chronicled the vicissitudes of that world with matchless understanding, wisdom, pity and truth, in the pages of this huge and marvellous book' – *Sunday Times*

Out of Africa   Karen Blixen (Isak Dinesen)

Karen Blixen went to Kenya in 1914 to run a coffee-farm; its failure in 1931 caused her to return to Denmark where she wrote this classic account of her experiences. 'A work of sincere power ... a fine lyrical study of life in East Africa' – Harold Nicolson in the *Daily Telegraph*

Yours Etc.   Graham Greene
Letters to the Press 1945–1989

'An entertaining celebration of Graham Greene's lesser-known career as a prolific author of letters to newspapers; you will find unarguable proof of his total addiction to everything about his time, from the greatest issues of the day to the humblest subjects imaginable' – Salman Rushdie in the *Observer*

The Trial of Lady Chatterley   Edited By C. H. Rolph

In October 1960 at the Old Bailey a jury of nine men and three women prepared for the infamous trial of *Lady Chatterley's Lover*. The Obscene Publications Act had been introduced the previous year and D. H. Lawrence's notorious novel was the first to be prosecuted under its provisions. This is the account of the historic trial and acquittal of Penguin Books.

Handbook for the Positive Revolution   Edward de Bono

Edward de Bono's challenging new book provides a practical framework for a serious revolution which has no enemies but seeks to make things better. The hand symbolizes the five basic principles of the Positive Revolution, to remind us that even a small contribution is better than endless criticism.

A CHOICE OF NON-FICTION

When Shrimps Learn to Whistle Denis Healey

Taking up the most powerful political themes that emerged from his hugely successful *The Time of My Life,* Denis Healey now gives us this stimulating companion volume. 'Forty-three years of ruminations ... by the greatest foreign secretary (as the author quietly and reasonably implies) we never had' – Ben Pimlott in the *New Statesman & Society*

Eastern Approaches Fitzroy Maclean

'The author's record of personal achievement is remarkable. The canvas which he covers is immense. The graphic writing reveals the ruthless man of action ... He emerges from [his book] as an extrovert Lawrence' – *The Times Literary Supplement*

This Time Next Week Leslie Thomas

'Mr Thomas's book is all humanity, to which is added a Welshman's mastery of words ... Some of his episodes are hilarious, some unbearably touching, but everyone, staff and children, is looked upon with compassion' – *Observer.* 'Admirably written, with clarity, realism, poignancy and humour' – *Daily Telegraph*

Reports from the Holocaust Larry Kramer

'A powerful book ... more than a political autobiography, *Reports* is an indictment of a world that allows AIDS to continue ... he is eloquent and convincing when he swings from the general to the specific. His recommendations on the release of drugs to AIDS patients are practical and humane' – *New York Newsday*

City on the Rocks Kevin Rafferty

'Rafferty has filled a glaring gap on the Asian bookshelf, offering the only comprehensive picture of Hong Kong right up to the impact of the Tiananmen Square massacre' – *Business Week.* 'A story of astonishing achievement, but its purpose is warning rather than celebration' – *Sunday Times*

READ MORE IN PENGUIN

A CHOICE OF NON-FICTION

The Time Out Film Guide   Edited by Tom Milne

The definitive, up-to-the minute directory of over 9,500 films – world cinema from classics and silent epics to reissues and the latest releases – assessed by two decades of *Time Out* reviewers. 'In my opinion the best and most comprehensive' – Barry Norman

The Remarkable Expedition   Olivia Manning

The events of an extraordinary attempt in 1887 to rescue Emin Pasha, Governor of Equatoria, are recounted here by the author of *The Balkan Trilogy* and *The Levant Trilogy* and vividly reveal unprecedented heights of magnificent folly in the perennial human search for glorious conquest.

Berlin: Coming in From the Cold   Ken Smith

'He covers everything from the fate of the ferocious-looking dogs that formerly helped to guard East Germany's borders to the vast Orwellian apparatus that maintained security in the now-defunct German Democratic Republic ... a pithy style and an eye for the telling detail' – *Independent*

Cider with Rosie/As I Walked Out one Midsummer Morning
Laurie Lee

Now together in one volume, Laurie Lee's two classic autobiographical works, *Cider with Rosie* and *As I Walked Out One Midsummer Morning*. Together they illustrate Laurie Lee's superb descriptive powers as he conveys the poignancy of a boy's transformation into adulthood.

In the Land of Oz   Howard Jacobson

'A wildly funny account of his travels; abounding in sharp characterization, crunching dialogue and self-parody, it actually is a book which makes you laugh out loud on almost every page ... sharp, skilful and brilliantly funny' – *Literary Review*

BY THE SAME AUTHOR

BERNARD SHAW

Volume 1: 1856–1898
The Search for Love

'The book touches the furthest boundaries of biography as an historical memoir of the years 1856–1898 in its unfolding of the details of Shaw's life: his Anglo-Irish middle-class poverty, his lively and eccentric relations, the mesmeric Vandeleur Lee . . . the passionate complexities leading up to his *mariage blanc*' – John Osborne in the *Spectator*

Volume 2: 1898–1918
The Pursuit of Power

'In addition to Shaw as playwright, Fabian, critic, musicologist, faddist, wag, nosy parker and philosopher, Mr Holroyd has brought his great work to a magnificent climax by giving us Shaw as hero' – Hugh Leonard in the *Irish Times*

Volume 3: 1918–1950
The Lure of Fantasy

'Shaw's vastness has met its match in the biographer's energy and power of synopsis . . . Holroyd's non-committal strategy is most striking in the descriptions of Shaw's infatuation with totalitarianism – the longest and most curious strand in this instalment of the life . . . a masterpiece of narrative efficiency' – John Sutherland in *The Times Literary Supplement*